Audio Editing with

Adobe Audition

Richard Riley

PC Publishing

PC Publishing
Keeper's House
Merton
Thetford
Norfolk IP25 6QH
UK

Tel +44 (0)1953 889900
email info@pc-publishing.com
website http://www.pc-publishing.com

First published 2008

ISBN 13: 978 1906005 030

British Library Cataloguing in Publication Data
A catalogue record for this book is available from the British Library

Printed and bound in Great Britain by Cromwell Press, Trowbridge, Wilts

Contents

Preface

This book is the third of a series of reference manuals for a little piece of software that I found in 1998 when looking for something to edit a Windows 95 startup sound. What was Cool Edit grew into Adobe Audition 1.5 and now Adobe Audition 2.0, the subject of this latest book.

Many people saw the Adobe purchase of Cool Edit as a bad thing for a piece of software that we'd all come to know very well. Adobe was treated with suspicion, after all didn't they just write software for the Mac? Since then Adobe has surprised us by developing Audition past 1.5 and into version 2.

Elements of the software exist as they always did. I smile when I see the Pitch Stretch effect looking almost exactly the same as with Cool Edit 2.0. But what Syntrillium didn't want to do Adobe have done. The adoption of ASIO brings a whole new audience, and the Multitrack View is now a professional working environment. Hopefully some of those people will look beyond simply what effects are available and will discover Adobe Audition for what it is; a truly useful, scientific audio tool with more depth than any other software at a comparable price.

I sincerely hope that this book will provide you with an insight into this remarkable software and the use of it in a changing world. I wish you peace as you enjoy making your music.

My thanks to the generosity of the members of the various forums and groups who have supported this book with their collective knowledge. Special thanks to Phil Chapman.

This book is dedicated to Jo, because I already owe her more than I know.

Richard Riley

Introduction

This book is laid out in three simple parts: The Multitrack View, Edit View and The CD View. Alongside these sections are further sections introducing the program and its features and key concepts of digital audio. Throughout the book are tips and tricks, general recording advice and hints on how to create and produce high quality music using nothing more than a reasonably priced laptop and a simple piece of software.

What's new in Adobe Audition 2.0

Adobe Audition 2.0 is a member of the Adobe Audio and Video product line. Other products in this line include Adobe Premiere, Photoshop and Flash. Adobe Audition 2.0 is the audio solution for use when creating professional audio productions and particularly for use in projects created in Flash or Premiere. Audio productions created in Adobe Audition 2.0 can also be used wherever professionally finished audio is required. The scientific and versatile nature of Adobe Audition means that it is used not only for the creation of commercial music but also for Film, Theatre, Radio and Contemporary music, Internet audio, streaming, podcasts and spoken word. Importantly; Adobe Audition audio clips can be any length and are not tied to a metronome or click. It is truly a tape recording environment without tape. Therefore, it is arguably a much better solution for spoken word and soundtrack creation than products created specifically to create music. On the other hand Adobe Audition will faultlessly synchronise with other MIDI and SMPTE equipped devices (via suitable adapters) to integrate with MIDI equipment.

Changes from Version 1.5

Adobe Audition 2.0 is almost a complete reworking of the Version 1.5 code, itself a rebadged version of Cool Edit Pro 2.1. One of the changes introduced during the reworking is that Version 2 now stores preferences and settings in XML documents. Previous versions of Adobe Audition used the registry to store preferences. This change brings Adobe Audition into line with other Adobe products such as Premiere and graphic design products such as InDesign and Photoshop. XML is a form of HTML, a plain text collection of tags and instructions which can be read by the host application in real time. XML files are small and easy to edit manually if necessary, unlike the more complex and system critical registry. This move to XML brings benefits and some drawbacks. XML files are simple to copy. This means that Adobe Audition preferences, effects settings and views can be copied from computer to computer with little difficulty. On the other hand XML seems to be a little more fragile than previously expected and a corrupt XML file will cause Adobe Audition to forget preferences. Whether this danger is real or perceived, most experienced Adobe Audition 2.0 users now regularly back preferences up. It's acknowledged that 2.0 is apparently a little more crash prone than previous versions.

Adobe Audition 2.0 now supports ASIO drivers, the Windows native WDM driver and Direct X 9. ASIO is a Steinberg technology created to enable low latency monitoring of instruments as they are recorded. without the need to use additional equipment such as mixing desks etc. As a side benefit recording using ASIO drivers also enables the performer to integrate VST real-time effects into the recording and listen to the VST effect as the performance is recorded and reproduced. Many thousands of free VST plugins have been developed and can be used at no cost. Adobe Audition introduced support for VST effects in Version 1.5 and this is continued through 2.0. Users can now bring their favourite effects or processors to Audition and use them in the same way as they were used in Cubase or Ableton Live etc. However, because Adobe Audition does not yet include the ability to record MIDI data, VST instruments cannot be used.

Significant changes

Adobe Audition 2.0 includes an additional CD view along with the traditional Edit and Multitrack view. CD printing (burning) features enable commercial production pre-mastering to be completed within Audition.

The multitrack view now includes a comprehensive mixer panel. Previous versions of Adobe Audition included a Mixer Window but this feature has been completely reworked to provide Adobe Audition with a complete mixer view containing familiar faders and switches.

Adobe Audition 2.0 no longer has the long running 'mix-gauge'. The introduction of real time effects through VST means that the mix gauge is redundant as the mix is now constantly rendered through the session.

Effects in the Adobe Audition mixer panel have been expanded dramatically. Adobe Audition is able to use native effects (processes), VST and Direct X in real time. There is also a Mastering Rack in the Edit View. This is the first version to include non-destructive effects in the Edit View.

Effects and other parameters can now be completely automated.

Flying panels containing folder lists, transport controls etc. can be docked anywhere inside the program, enabling a personal workspace to be created. In particular, panels can be docked behind panels.

Adobe Audition and other Adobe media products

The high-quality professional audio editing tools in Adobe Audition are a great match for the video professional. Adobe Production Studio Premium users can use the Edit in Adobe Audition command in either After Effects or Adobe Premiere Pro to quickly launch Adobe Audition when you want to edit any audio clip or the audio component of any video clip, regardless of the clip's original authoring application. After your edits are complete, save the file in Adobe Audition and it will automatically update in After Effects or Adobe Premiere Pro. Users can import AVI, MPEG, native digital video (DV), and Windows Media Video (WMV) files; video tracks appear with multiple thumbnails, making it easy to synchronize audio with specific frames in the video.

Markers in Adobe Premiere Pro 2.0 AVI files import into Adobe Audition. Built-in looping tools and royalty-free loop content are perfect for sound bed creation, and powerful noise reduction tools are great for cleaning up poor-quality audio, including unwanted noise from wireless microphones and DV cameras. Adobe Audition can also be used for dialog replacement, sound effects, sweetening, mixing, and many other aspects of video soundtrack creation. Users can also import audio (WAV) files into Adobe Premiere Pro or After Effects projects, and then use the Edit Original command to open either the WAV or session file (requires After Effects 6.0 or later) in Adobe Audition, and VST effects can be shared between Adobe Premiere Pro 2.0 and Adobe Audition 2.0.

Key concepts

Audio manipulation and production program all share a few simple concepts. Understanding what digital audio is, and how computers can record and reproduce music and speech is crucial to getting the best out of Adobe Audition 2.0.

Digital audio

Digital audio is required anytime that a computer needs to make a sound. Applications for digital audio include broadcasting; digital TV or radio, home entertainment; iPod, or CD player etc. and internet streaming; MySpace, Youtube. Other applications include mobile phone technology and of course multi-media and music production. Adobe Audition can be used to create and edit audio for all of these applications.

Sound is digitised by the soundcard, not the program. For high quality results use a professional sound card. Adobe Audition 2.0 can't rescue a poorly sampled or recorded clip

When sound is recorded it is stored as data in files stored inside the computer. Files stored in some ways (Wav, Au, Aiff etc.) can be accessed and changed by many different applications. Some programs store sound in formats that cannot be opened by all programs.

The audible clarity of the digitised sound is determined by the sampling rate and bit depth used to record the sound. Lower sample rates and bit depth can only produce inferior quality recordings.

Sound recorded using high sample rates and bit depth are high quality because they contain a large amount of information about the source material. These files are larger and are much more intensive for the computer. Therefore manipulating sound data recorded or stored at high sample rates requires a more powerful computer.

When sound is digitised it is rendered into data. The data is handled in the same way as any other data inside the computer. That it, the computer stores and finds the files used to hold the information needed to reproduce the audio and the central processing unit inside the computer manages the calculations and instructions required to turn that data back into audio. The performance of the host computer governs the ability of the programs installed. Adobe Audition is not a processor intensive application until effects and processors are used in real time. If you can manage without real-time effects you will find that Adobe Audition 2.0 will run on an Intel processor based computer running at a minimum of 800mHz and with at least 256mb of ram. At least 500mb of free space is required for the program files and temporary files. Additional storage space is required for any files you may create.

In addition, a soundcard is required for the recording and playback of digital audio. It's uncommon now to find a computer without a built-in soundcard although additional equipment will be required for multi-channel professional results. The soundcard can be fitted internally or may have a USB or Firewire interface.

A much more powerful computer is required when using real-time effects and particularly if using Video. These are the minimum requirements for Adobe Audition as published by Adobe.

- Intel® Pentium® III or 4 or Intel Centrino™ (or other SSE-enabled) processor (Pentium 4 or other SSE2-enabled processor required for video)
- Microsoft® Windows® XP Professional or Home Edition with Service Pack 2
- 512MB of RAM (1GB recommended)
- 700MB of available hard-disk space (5.5GB recommended for installing optional audio clips)
- 1,024x768 display (1,280x1,024 recommended)
- Sound card with DirectSound or ASIO drivers (multitrack ASIO sound card recommended)
- CD-ROM drive (DVD-ROM drive recommended for installing optional audio clips)
- CD-RW drive for audio CD creation
- Speakers or headphones recommended
- Internet or phone connection required for product activation and Internet-related services

A computer with these components will support Adobe Audition 2.0 but may not manage your choice of real–time VST or Direct X effects. Other Adobe Audition features such as Automation and Video or MIDI clips will also increase the load on the host computer. The following table suggests specifications for a computer able to support a number of VST and Direct X effects in a fully automated multi-clip session.

- Intel® Pentium® Dual Core or better
- Microsoft Windows Vista Home Premium or Microsoft® Windows® XP Professional with Service Pack 2

- 2GB of RAM
- 700MB of available hard-disk space (250GB recommended for installing optional audio clips)
- Dual Widescreen TFT 1,024x768 display (1,280x1,024 recommended)
- Sound card with DirectSound or ASIO drivers (multitrack ASIO sound card recommended)
- DVD Read/Writer
- CD-RW drive for audio CD creation
- Internal Speakers or headphones recommended for system sounds only
- Professional 24/96 sound card with multi-i/o, SP-DIF
- MIDI interface
- Internet or phone connection required for product activation and Internet-related services
- High speed DSL connection

Performance expectations

The following table is an adapted extract from the documentation provided for users of Adobe Audition 2.0 by Adobe.

The performance you may expect from your computer running Adobe Audition 2.0 is unique to you, your environment and the ways in which you prefer to work. Because of this, it is almost impossible to produce accurate predictions for the sort of performance you may expect from Adobe Audition 2.0. Many people judge system performance on the amount of real time effects and processors that a host system can support, without crashing or suffering critical loss of control. However not all effects and processes are equal. Factors affecting the load on the PC caused by the use of real time effects include the type of effect, the ability of the developer and the nature of the processes used by the effect to produce the required result.

A number of effects and processes are bundled with Adobe Audition 2.0. Each of these has been created and designed to minimise the load on the host computer. They can all be used as real time effects in conjunction with other effects. The following table groups these 'native' effects by processor load.

High
Multiband Compressor, Chorus, Full Reverb, Reverb, Center Channel Extractor, Notch Filter, Pitch Shifter.

Medium
Dynamics Processing, Flanger, Multitap Delay, Studio Reverb, Graphic EQ, Distortion.

Low
Hard Limiter, Echo, Graphic Phase Shifter, Parametric EQ.

Minimal
Track EQ, Tube Modeled Compressor*, Amplify, Channel Mixer, Delay, Stereo Expander, Stereo Field Rotate, Delay, Sweeping Phaser.

Effects in the high load group can be used in real time but for optimal performance should not be combined with other effects in effects racks etc. If possible, consider using these effects as a post-production tool such as in the Edit View mastering rack and applied to the entire waveform

Effects in the medium load group may be used in the multitrack view and can be combined with other effects but for best performance should be used in mixer tracks and then frozen.

Effects in the Low group can be used freely in the multitrack view in real time

Effects in the minimal group can be chained and combined many times in the multitrack view and are the best choice if choosing effects for external monitoring.

Installation and activation

Adobe Audition is distributed as a single program. It is available as a download from adobe.com or a retail boxed product. Currently Adobe Audition 2.0 is not available as part of the Adobe Creative Suite. The installation routine follows Microsoft conventions for an installer program. Should Adobe Audition stall during installation, or should the program not finish the installation routine, check the following on your computer:

- Adobe Audition 2.0 is designed for Windows XP. It has been tested. successfully with Windows Vista. Adobe Audition 2.0 is not available for Apple Macintosh.
- Check that you have sufficient disk space. You will need at least 700mb of free space, and additional space for large temporary files.
- Check that you have a minimum of 512MB physical memory
- Your display settings must be at least 1024 x 768 and true colour.
- Your graphics card and soundcard have Vista or XP compatible drivers.
- Remove USB storage devices and USB license 'dongles'.

Always install Adobe Audition 2.0 after finally installing and configuring soundcard and graphics devices. Adobe Audition will detect hardware on start up and configure accordingly. A working internet connection is required for the program to be able to activate automatically. After installation Adobe Audition will attempt to activate automatically via the internet. If it is unable to find a working internet connection it will prompt you to call Adobe and activate over the phone. A valid license key is required for activation. Without a valid license key the program will function for 30 days.

File locations

Adobe Audition 2.0 will detect available storage devices and will prompt for the location of two temporary folders. These folders will contain temporary files created during normal running of the program.

If possible locate the temp and session files on different physical disks. The best place for the temporary file is on a large hard disk, away from the physical disk containing the system and program files. The second temporary file can be placed on the system disk if necessary as it will only become used if the first disk is full.

During installation Adobe Audition will offer to become the default program for a number of file types. Choose file types depending on your personal requirements. For instance configuring Adobe Audition as the default handler for .mp3 files may cause other player programs such as Napster to stop working. Always enable Adobe Audition as the default handler for .wav files.

After the installation is complete you will be prompted to register your copy of Adobe Audition over the internet. Registration provides access to a complimentary telephone support line for fault related calls (not 'how to' or calls related to third party plug in effects) and places you in line for any relevant upgrades.

Adobe Audition 2.0 will load the default session; Audition-Theme Session on first run. Use this session to experiment with Audition. The Adobe theme session is loaded from C:\Program Files\Adobe\Adobe Audition 2.0\Audition Theme

Session folders

During every session wave files are stored in a folder underneath the location of the session file. For instance a session file called newsong.ses is stored in d:\mysongs. Adobe Audition 2.0 will automatically create another folder called d:\mysongs\newsong_recorded. This folder will be used to contain all the recorded material created in that session. For this reason you should try to make sure that the temporary folder is not located on the same physical disk as the session files and folders. Adobe Audition 2.0 no longer requires that files recorded during the session are named before saving. Instead the files are automatically named and saved into the session folder.

Files are named according to the following convention:

[TrackName]_[FileNumber] (duplicate number).(duplicate number)

Therefore,

Guitar_009 The ninth recording in the session. This recording was made in the Guitar track
Guitar_009 (2)   The second duplicate of the Guitar_009 track
Guitar_009 (2.1) The first copy of the second duplication of Guitar 009

All the files created in the session, including clips duplicated and unique clips are named in the file panel. Right click over any of these files to see further options.

Other components installed with Adobe Audition 2.0

Along with Audition, the installer program installs the Adobe Bridge program. This is a handler and file management program intended to make file sharing easier among Adobe products. It is intended to link Adobe products, such as the Adobe Creative suite together. The Adobe bridge includes some useful tools such as the batch rename function and the ability to view and edit detailed file information. However, it is most useful when used as a connector for many Adobe products installed on the one computer.

XP and Windows Vista performance tweaks

Adobe Audition 2.0 will run fine straight out of the box on nearly any computer bought in the last eight years. The core program at the heart of Adobe Audition was developed in the early nineties and was known to be the most robust audio application available for the PC. Adobe Audition has grown since then and the inclusion of VST and Direct X effects brings additional load on the processor and supporting hardware. Any benefits obtained from lessening operating system load on the computer will translate into additional power for Adobe Audition and should therefore be considered if your system is unable to support the real time effects that you need.

Add more RAM
Vista is the most memory hungry operating system that Microsoft has ever produced. Complex 64 bit applications and memory hungry desktop themes such as Aero eat up system resources like never before. Adobe Audition 2.0 likes as much memory as it can get – a minimum of 2GB for complex multi-clip sessions with video and real time effects

Add an additional monitor
A fast graphics card with dual monitor outs will increase performance in two ways. Firstly, a quality graphics card will add power to your computer. Secondly, an additional monitor will enable you to take advantage of the dual monitor workspace presets in Adobe Audition. A dual monitor present places the multitrack session in one monitor and the mixer panel in the other monitor. This will help you work faster in Adobe Audition and make your time in the program more enjoyable.

Disable or remove unnecessary visual effects
Some computers have built in graphics cards that are impossible to upgrade. If your system is suffering from slow graphics performance, turn off the default Vista visual effects that while looking pretty, can slow down your system.

To disable visual effects find the Vista Performance information and Tools applet. Type 'performance' in the search bar and click on the applet in the list of found items. From within the Performance information dialogue box click on the item 'Adjust Visual Effects' from the list on the left. This dialogue presents a list of features which can be added or removed to fine tune your system. Or simply choose the option to 'Adjust For Best Performance'.

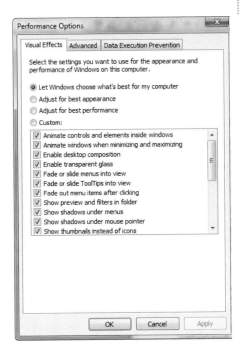

Choosing this option will remove all Vista visual effects and replace the current theme with the windows classic theme. However your system will become much more responsive.

Hard disk maintenance (XP and Vista)

Audio makes critical demands on your hard disk. Files have to be written and data has to be read in real time, a world away from the task of say – storing the words that make up this book. HDD performance is therefore critical.

Always defragment your hard disk once a week. Make it into a housekeeping task. Data that is fragmented is stored in small parts, all over the surface of the disk. Finding this data then becomes and additional task for the computer. Defragmenting the hard disk involves asking the computer to find and join up all these little bits of data so that future disk accesses will be

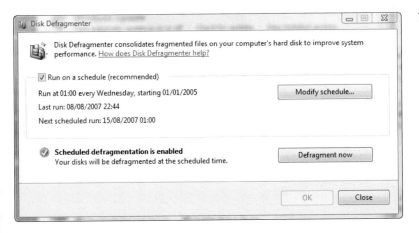

The disk defragmentation tool

much quicker. The disk defragmentation tool is found in the control panel, system maintenance dialogue in the section 'Administrative Tools'

Disable unwanted applications at startup (XP and Vista)

Although third party applications may not slow down your computer during the session, it's likely that some unwanted programs will have added themselves to the list of programs that autoload immediately after the operating system has started. Add-ins for Internet Explorer, Instant Messaging and applications designed to detect mal-ware will add greatly to the time it takes your PC to get up and running. You can detect and disable these programs n many ways. One of the simplest ways to do this is simply to use the Microsoft configuration utility 'msconfig'. Type 'msconfig' in the XP run box

Use the Microsoft configuration utility 'msconfig' to disable unwanted programs

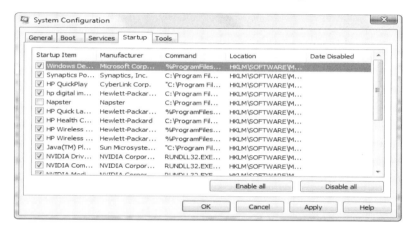

or in the Vista search field. Vista will prompt for UAC (User Access Control) but this is normal. Within msconfig disable unwanted programs by deselecting them in the list of startup items.

Another option is to use Autoruns by Mark Russinovich (http://www.sysinternals.com) Autoruns finds all items configured to run at startup, including the ones missed in the Microsoft utility. It also provides an option to delete, once you are sure that they are completely unwanted.

Anti-virus and anti-spam software

Anti-virus and anti-spam software has its place, but not on a computer that is well built, well maintained and most importantly – well used and protected. Anti-spam 'suites' contain layers of software devices which are intended to provide defences against common internet borne attacks such as internet 'worms', spyware and adware. These require large amounts of system resources and slow down powerful systems. A properly maintained DAW which is behind an efficient firewall and is used sensibly will remain free of attack. Follow these simple guidelines when operating your DAW in this way.

Remove Norton, McAfee and other malware 'suite' programs. Leave the Windows firewall in place and enabled. Make sure that Windows defender is enabled and up to date.

Enable Windows firewall on all other desktops and laptops on the LAN

Do not use your DAW when reading your email. In particular, never download email attachments to the DAW. 90% of malware arrive on your computer through email attachments

---

Info

In every 100 emails travelling from computer to computer, approximately ten will be useful content intended for the recipient alone. 20 of the remaining 90 emails will contain virus code. The remaining 70 emails will be automatically generated spam hoping to reach email addresses either harvested from poorly secured servers, gathered from forums and webpages or simply made up.

Use a router and firewall. Do not use cheap USB modems for your DSL (broadband connection). USB modems do not have firewall technology and can be enabled remotely by spyware and internet worm virus.

Plug your PC into the private port of your Ethernet router/modem and configure your router before attaching it to the DSL enabled phone line. It can take just 20 seconds for a unprotected computer to become infected with internet bourne virus code. Close every external Wan -> LAN port on the router and always use NAT, never use a public IP address on the private side of the router. Check your router security at http://www.grc.com.

GRC's examination of my own system

Port	Service	Status	Security Implications
0	<nil>	Stealth	There is NO EVIDENCE WHATSOEVER that a port (or even any computer) exists at this IP address!
21	FTP	Stealth	There is NO EVIDENCE WHATSOEVER that a port (or even any computer) exists at this IP address!
22	SSH	Stealth	There is NO EVIDENCE WHATSOEVER that a port (or even any computer) exists at this IP address!
23	Telnet	Stealth	There is NO EVIDENCE WHATSOEVER that a port (or even any computer) exists at this IP address!
25	SMTP	Stealth	There is NO EVIDENCE WHATSOEVER that a port (or even any computer) exists at this IP address!
79	Finger	Stealth	There is NO EVIDENCE WHATSOEVER that a port (or even any computer) exists at this IP address!
80	HTTP	Stealth	There is NO EVIDENCE WHATSOEVER that a port (or even any computer) exists at this IP address!
110	POP3	Stealth	There is NO EVIDENCE WHATSOEVER that a port (or even any computer) exists at this IP address!
113	IDENT	Stealth	There is NO EVIDENCE WHATSOEVER that a port (or even any computer) exists at this IP address!
119	NNTP	Stealth	There is NO EVIDENCE WHATSOEVER that a port (or even any computer) exists at this IP address!
135	RPC	Stealth	There is NO EVIDENCE WHATSOEVER that a port (or even any computer) exists at this IP address!
139	Net BIOS	Stealth	There is NO EVIDENCE WHATSOEVER that a port (or even any computer) exists at this IP address!

This extract from GRC's examination of my own system indicates that no ports are available externally. This means that my system is invisible from the internet. This is exactly what I want.

Readyboost (Vista only)

Microsoft Readyboost is a new feature of Windows Vista that attempts to aid users with low powered PC's who want to use Vista. Microsoft enables Vista to save page files to low price removable storage devices such as USB 'sticks' or SD cards. Because solid state memory (NAND) devices have no moving parts they can in some cases have higher read/write speeds than conventional hard disk drives. In addition, the advantages of storing data on a different device than the page file also becomes available. In reality the performance benefits are slight.

Only the most expensive USB 2.0 devices have access speeds anywhere near what is required for tangible performance benefits compared to the marginal cost of additional hard disks. However, laptop users can see a slight benefit, especially as laptops are much harder and more expensive to upgrade. In this case the more expensive USB drives become cheaper than laptop parts and so the minor performance boost becomes more cost effective. For Adobe Audition the performance benefits are even more marginal. Temp directories should not be placed on USB memory as Adobe Audition constantly needs to write to .pk files. But if you are having performance issues with Adobe Audition on a Vista equipped laptop, Readyboost may give you just enough headroom to continue.

Microsoft Readyboost attempts to aid users with low powered PC's who want to use Vista.

To use Readyboost simply insert a USB removable memory device, or SD-Card into the Vista Laptop. Vista will examine the device and if possible will place an additional option in the Device Found prompt. The device should not be removed until the laptop has shut down completely.

Configuring Adobe Audition

After installation Adobe Audition is ready to use. For many people the preferences and settings created during installation will support all they need from the program. However, users with more demanding projects should examine the available preferences and ensure that Adobe Audition 2.0 is optimised for the way that you work.

Audio preferences

On installation Adobe Audition detects installed soundcards. Therefore it is important to have your hardware installed correctly before installing Adobe Audition. Check and configure your devices using Audio Hardware Setup from the Edit menu in either the multitrack or edit view.

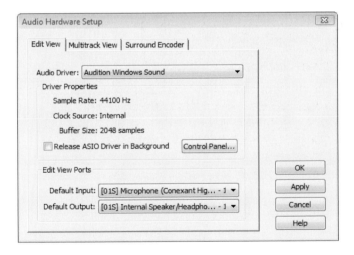

Check and configure your devices using Audio Hardware Setup.

Edit View
Choose either the Audition Windows Sound (WDM) driver or an ASIO driver. The default inputs and outputs are used in Edit View

Multitrack view
Choose the ASIO driver if possible for minimum latency. The default inputs and outputs will be used by the Mixer Panel on startup but can be changed from the track properties.

Surround encoder

A 5.1 or 7.1 decoder must be installed for proper decoding and reproduction of surround sound audio. If the decoder is not fitted Adobe Audition will reproduce surround sound as stereo through these device outputs.

Tip

Some drivers cannot be used by more than one application at a time. The three parts to this dialogue box look like three applications to these drivers and you may find that the edit view or multitrack view stops responding if the same driver is chosen for both. Use the WDM driver until new soundcard drivers can be installed.

Adobe Audition will detect soundcards with ASIO capability. The option to use the ASIO driver will then appear in each of the hardware tabs. If possible always use the ASIO driver as this will not only produce the lowest latency times, but will enable additional features from the soundcards own control panel. If your soundcard driver does not have ASIO drivers use the ASIO4ALL driver from

http://www.asio4all.com

If possible always use the ASIO driver.

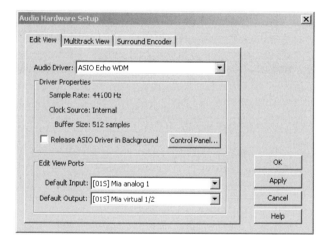

There may be occasions when the ASIO driver may not function correctly. To enable soundcards with incompatible drivers, and to provide backwards compatibility with cards that use WDM drivers (Adobe Audition 1.5 could not support ASIO and therefore the upgrade to 2.0 may have left some people unable to use the new version) Audition also creates an alternative driver entitled 'Audition Windows Sound'. The Audition Windows Sound uses the Microsoft Direct Sound API, a component of Direct X. This is a very stable and reliable driver for Adobe Audition but it has high latency and is unsuitable for the Audition Mix feature. Only external monitoring is suitable for use with Direct Sound.

Soundcards without ASIO drivers are supported in Adobe Audition 2.0 with the Audition Windows Sound feature.

Enhancing soundcard performance using preferences

Adobe Audition will install Audition Windows Sound with a set of default parameters. Usually, the default parameters do not need to be adjusted as a performance computer with a quality soundcard will be capable of providing a comfortable recording and playback environment. If you need to use the Audition Mix feature, you may find that adjusting parameters such as buffer size will increase Adobe Audition performance. Changes in buffer size and other settings for ASIO cards must be done through the ASIO control panel included in the Audio Hardware Preferences dialog.

Tip

W arning. Proceed with caution. Entering the wrong settings here may cause Adobe Audition to perform badly. Make a note of every setting before changing it.

Direct Sound buffer size

Latency can be reduced by reducing the number of buffers that are used. Audition requests wave data in buffers from the soundcard. By retrieving the buffers before they are required Adobe Audition is able to seamlessly create playback without interruption from other applications or the operating system. If the number of buffers is lowered, the audio will appear to reach Adobe Audition in more or less real time. However this leaves no room for errors introduced by poor hard disk performance etc. and so performance may suffer. Lowering buffer size also slows loading multitrack sessions and waveforms.

Raise or lower the number of buffers in the Audio Hardware Setup dialog box. With the 'Audition Windows Sound' driver chosen, click the button marked 'Control Panel'.

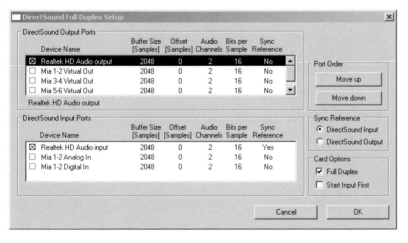

Raise or lower the number of buffers in the Audio Hardware Setup dialog.

Check the box next to the audio input that you wish to edit and select the buffer settings using the mouse, the buffer settings can be overtyped using the keyboard. If you are experiencing high latency issues, experiment by lowering the buffer size. The default buffer size setting is 2048 buffers. Settings of 32 to 256 buffers will decrease your latency at the expense of performance. On the other hand, increasing the buffer size with produce seamless audio but latency will increase to the point where only the external monitoring setting is useful.

Remove unused devices. Within the Direct Sound control panel there is also the option to deselect direct sound devices. While this won't have any effect on your system resources, Adobe Audition won't list unused devices which will make your workspace tider.

Wave cache

Adobe Audition stores some waveform information in RAM as wave cache. Because RAM memory has much faster read/write access times than Hard Disk memory data stored here can very quickly be read by the program and translated into waveform display. The amount of data stored in the wave cache has a relation to the amount of physical RAM installed in your computer.

Installed RAM	Recommended Wave Cache Setting
512MB	32MB
1GB	64MB
2GB	128MB

The Wave Cache preference is in Adobe Audition system settings. Choose Edit, Preferences (or press Function F4) then System. Enter the new figure and press OK. Adobe Audition will use the new settings on the next restart.

Choose Edit, Preferences then System. Enter the new figure and press OK.

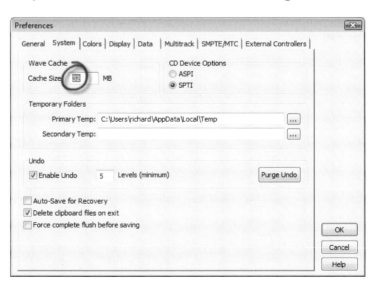

General Adobe Audition preferences

Adobe Audition has a number of user editable preferences. Preferences can be changed to configure Adobe Audition to suit your environment. It's important not to casually change preferences as you can harm the performance of the program. Always make a note of the default preferences before editing.

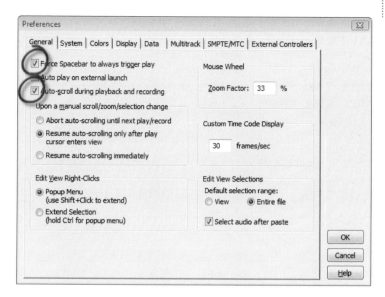

Always make a note of the default preferences before editing.

Force spacebar. When using the mixer or in effects racks the spacebar will always start and stop the transport.

Auto Scroll. Adobe Audition will scroll the multitrack window from right to left when playing and recording. This can be defeated by deselecting this check box.

CD Device Options. If you have a SCSI CD drive choose the ASPI (Advanced SCSI Programming Interface) option. Otherwise choose SPTI (SCSI Pass Through Interface)

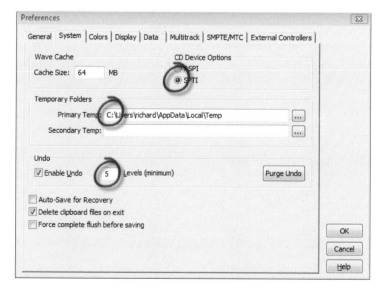

CD device options.

Temporary folders. This is the location of the temporary folders. By default Adobe Audition will choose your largest fixed disk although this can be changed here.

Enable undo. This figure configures the minimum number of actions that you can undo. The default setting of five provides five backward steps using Edit, Undo. You may raise this figure but more levels will have an effect on system performance as changes are stored in memory until flushed. You can retrieve memory in emergency by Purging the Undo store. This will reduce memory load if Adobe Audition performance is critical.

Colour scheme. If you prefer, you may choose a different colour scheme using the options in the Colours tab. The most useful tool here is the UI (User Interface) brightness control. This enables you to dim the Adobe Audition 2.0 GUI (Graphical User Interface), extremely useful for instance when using Adobe Audition 2.0 in a dim control booth in a dark theatre. Note that the only control to effect the Adobe Audition Multitrack visuals is the UI brightness control. Colour schemes are applied to the edit view only.

Choose a different colour scheme using the options in the Colours tab.

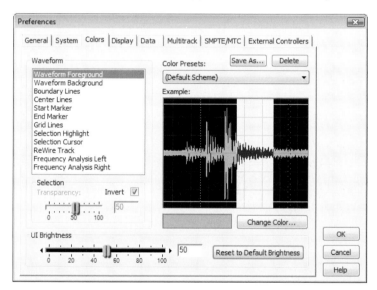

Peak Files. Peak information is stored for every waveform when Adobe Audition draws it for the first time. Then when the waveform is loaded again, Adobe Audition is able to very quickly redraw the waveform without scanning the file each time. If you have a limited amount of physical memory, you may find that increasing the number of samples per block (effectively lowering the resolution) will reduce the amount of memory required. This is most effective when working with very large waveforms of more than 500MB in size. Increase the Peaks Cache, doubling each time; 1024 or a maximum or 2048.

Save Peak Cache Files. Deselect this option to completely disable the peaks cache feature. This could save some disk space although Peak Cache files are tiny and fast drawing of waveforms is vital.

Rebuild wave display. Sometimes, Adobe Audition may display waveforms incorrectly or may refuse to draw an entire waveform. If this happens, choose

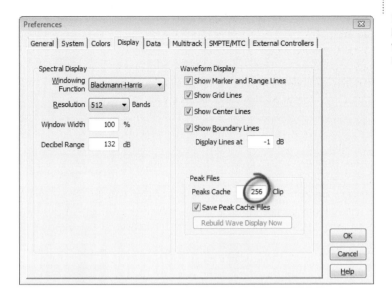

Increasing the number of samples per block (effectively lowering the resolution) will reduce the amount of memory required.

to rebuild the wave display. This will recreate the peak file (.pk) associated with this waveform.

The data tab of the preferences window contains controls relating to how Adobe Audition processes data when recording and transforming data.

The data tab of the preferences window contains controls relating to how Adobe Audition processes data.

Info

Effects were called 'Transforms' in early versions of Adobe Audition. Some parts of the program still refer to transforms. Transformed data is data that has been processed by an Adobe Audition native process effect.

Most of these preferences should be left as installed. Adobe Audition is designed to produce high quality audio and the controls here are set to the optimum. One exception for this may be the downsampling quality level. Because most recordings are now done in the 24/96 domain, downsampling to 16 bit is necessary when creating a Red-Book CD (16/44). The down-sampling quality level setting enables control over the weighting of high level frequencies during this process. In general, a high setting creates more high frequencies. Because this will affect the way your waveform will sound after downsampling, you may wish to experiment with different settings depending on your program. Higher values produce more high frequencies. Lowering the values can produce a dull result. The default setting is 80. Experiment with values between 80 and 400. Only raise the value above 400 if you wish to produce an unusual effect!

Multitrack preferences. These controls produce the defaults used when recording in the multitrack view. For best results leave the recording bit depth and the bounce bit depth to 32bit. Change this to the lower 16 bit only if your system is experiencing critical system degradation, such as when managing large numbers of 24/96 clips in a session with many real time effects.

Stereo panning mode enables you to choose between logarithmic or equal-power panning. Logarithmic panning produces a cut in volume when panning right or left as the waveform volume is attenuated. Equal Power panning sums both channels of the stereo waveform to either side. This produces a +3db peak when panned 100% left or right.

Ensure that Auto Zero Cross edits is selected. This will prevent audible pops and clicks appearing whenever clips are joined togther. Ensure that smooth scrolling is enabled.

Multitrack preferences produce the defaults used when recording in the multitrack view.

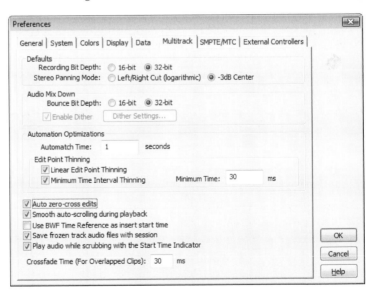

SMPTE preferences control the behaviour of Adobe Audition when acting as a SMPTE slave or master. Adobe Audition can control other devices using SMPTE over MTC. When acting as a slave it may be necessary to edit these preferences in order to compensate for variable code quality, system performance etc.

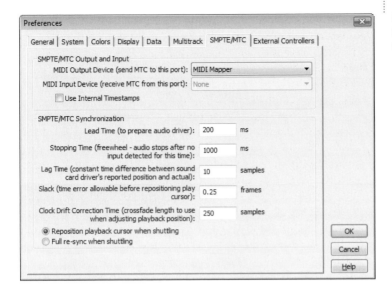

SMPTE preferences control the behaviour of Adobe Audition when acting as a SMPTE slave or master.

Lead Time. This is the amount of time that Adobe Audition will stall while the audio is prepared after a start signal is received via timecode. Use higher values for slower systems

Stopping Time. Sets the amount of play left in Adobe Audition after a stop signal is received.

Lag Time. Allows for latency by providing an offset in samples. Experiment with higher values if you have a high latency soundcard.

Slack. Adobe Audition will drift slightly while acting as a slave. Use this control to set how far you are prepared to let Adobe Audition drift before forcing a reposition. Lower settings may produce a jerky response as the playback is constantly corrected.

Clock Drift Correction. Sets the number of samples used to crossfade when correcting playback position.

External controllers such as the Mackie MCU Pro and compatible controllers (Yamaha 01X) can be used to control Adobe Audition. The External Controllers window presents the control panel for your chosen device if available. Currently only a small number of controllers are supported in Audition. At time of writing drivers for Adobe Audition are available for controllers from Mackie, Tascam and Frontier Design. Contact the manufacturer of your controller for more information.

MIDI preferences
Adobe Audition 2.0 has simple MIDI file player features. Audition cannot sequence and is not able to record or edit MIDI data. MIDI preferences enable control over MIDI playback devices.

Adobe Audition detects installed MIDI devices. Enable or disable devices by adding or removing them from the list of active MIDI devices.

Rewire

Adobe Audition will host Rewire sessions active on the same computer. Rewire is a routing plug-in developed by Propellerhead Software. A Rewire host such as Adobe Audition can function as a mixer for Rewire enabled synth applications on the same computer. This enables Adobe Audition to become a hub for Rewire applications, MIDI and Video files and any wav or loop files in the same session.

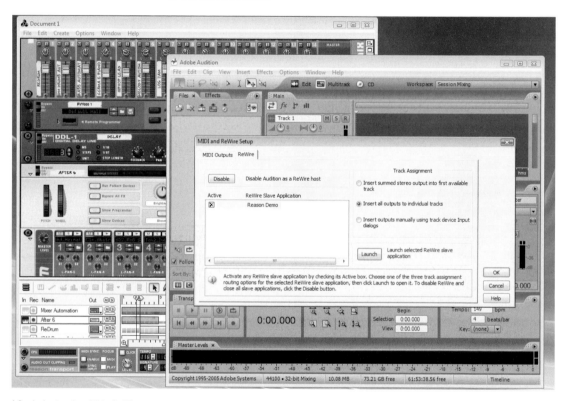

A Rewire host such as Adobe Audition can function as a mixer for Rewire enabled synth applications on the same computer.

Install the Rewire synth and create a new session for your Rewire enabled project before enabling Rewire in Adobe Audition. Rewire enabled applications will appear in the list of applications in the Rewire tab of the MIDI setup dialog. Choose one of the three track assignment options. Rewire hosts can offer many outputs to Adobe Audition. Although the session can accommodate hundreds of Tracks it can easily become confusing to have multiple Rewire instruments. The option to sum all tracks conveniently brings all Rewire outputs into one stereo track and allows mixing to be handled in the Rewire synth application.

When the Rewire synth is active click the Launch button. The active Rewire application will launch. Start and stop the selected Rewire application using the Adobe Audition transport controls. Tempo is controlled by Adobe Audition and set at the session properties.

Keyboard shortcuts and MIDI triggers

Adobe Audition can be controlled using MIDI or keyboard shortcuts. Shortcut keys are keyboard combinations which will trigger an event or procedure within Adobe Audition. Some of the principal commands such as adding to the marker list (F8) are already enabled.

To create a shortcut pick the action required from the list and click in the field called 'create new shortcut key'. Press the shortcut key or combination of keys. This will be saved alongside the command name.

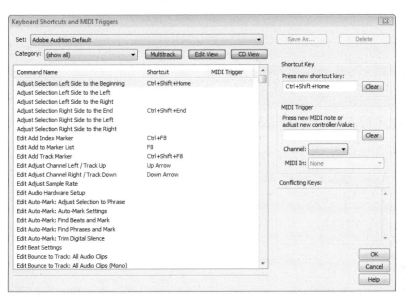

To create a shortcut pick the action required from the list and click in the field called 'create new shortcut key'.

MIDI triggers

MIDI triggering is used to control Adobe Audition from any MIDI device. When used in this way, Adobe Audition can be controlled by a MIDI keyboard or even a sequencer or MIDI file player. In this way Adobe Audition can be incorporated into a fully automated MIDI controlled playback system. Systems like this are commonly created to control and automate theatrical shows or complex rock events.

Create a new MIDI trigger using the MIDI triggers preferences (Edit, keyboard Shortcuts and MIDI triggers or AltK). Select a new command and click inside the 'new MIDI note' field. Ensure that the MIDI in device is selected and press a key on the MIDI keyboard or use a controller to generate MIDI information. Adobe Audition will analyse incoming information and apply the trigger to the selected command.

Workspaces, Panels and Tabs

One of the most noticeable developments in Adobe Audition 2.0 is the appearance of layered tabs and panels. Previous versions of Adobe Audition had difficulty accommodating the large number of windows needed during a busy session. Adobe Audition 2.0 resolves this difficulty by producing a 3D workspace. Not only are panels laid up and across the screen, panels can also be layered behind each other and appear as tabs.

Workspaces

A collection of panels, tabs and windows is called a Workspace. Multiple workspaces may be created and saved for different applications. Adobe Audition comes with a preset selection of workspaces, some designed to make use of twin monitor systems.

To create your own workspace. Open move and arrange windows and panels. When you are satisfied choose Window, Workspace, New Workspace from the menu bar. Your workspace will be saved and available from the Workspace menu.

To delete a workspace. With the workspace in view choose Window, Workspace, Delete Workspace.

This is a very busy Edit window containing a single mono file. Notice the multiple panels appearing as tabs. Click on the small triangle at the right corner to dock or undock the panel. Undocked panels are floating windows which may be moved right outside the application window. Ctrl+Shift+F12 will return the workspace to its default.

This is a very busy Edit window containing a single mono file. Notice the multiple panels appearing as tabs.

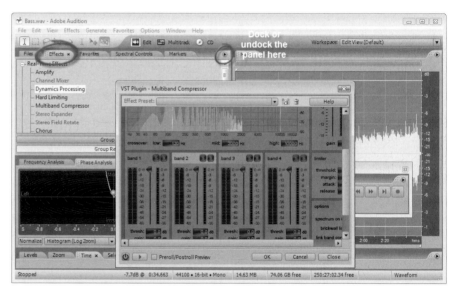

Docking and undocking panels

A panel is a view that is docked into the current workspace. When more than one panel occupies the same area of the screen it is hidden behind the current panel. When this happens the panel becomes hidden except for a small tab appearing above the foremost panel.

To undock a panel click on the small twistie on the top rightmost part of the panel. Choose undock panel to release the panel. The panel then appears in a floating window. Redock the floating panel by clicking on the section to the left of the panel name a dragging this onto a currently docked panel.

Groups of panels can be undocked using the undock frame option.

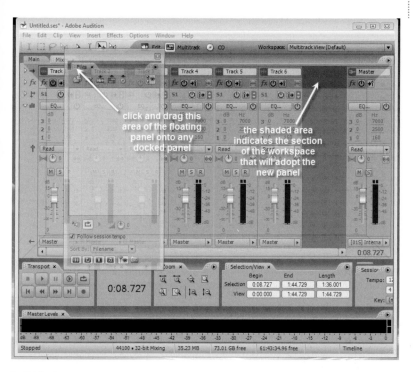

To undock a panel click on the small twistie on the top rightmost part of the panel. Choose undock panel to release the panel. The panel then appears in a floating window.

Individual panels

Each panel houses a group of controls. Use combinations of panels to create individual workspaces.

The mixer panel provides track controls in a familiar mixer form.

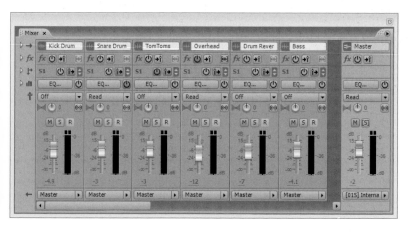

The mixer panel.

Top to bottom this column:
The files panel, the effects panel and the favourites panel.

The files panel is an explorer style window. Files can be dragged and dropped from here onto the multitrack session. The file can also be previewed using the auditioning controls at the base of the panel. Use the file types filter button to mask files of a particular type.

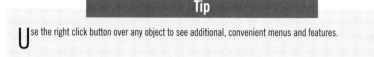

U se the right click button over any object to see additional, convenient menus and features.

The Effects panel. Process effects and VST effects are shown in this window. Effects can be dragged onto multitrack tracks from here. Effects can also be grouped by category.

The Favourites panel. Favourites are most often used effects and processes. You can create your own favourites from almost any Audition feature or effect. Click the Edit Favourites button to reveal the Favourites control panel. Give your new favourite a name and assign a shortcut key. From the tabbed options choose an existing Adobe Audition effect, script or third party tool.

The Level Meter displays stereo or mono levels. Hard right is 0dBfs. Right click on the level meters to see range and peak options.

The time window (right) accurately shows track length in elapsed time, bars and beats, samples etc. Decimal time is the default. Right click for options.

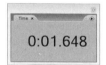

The transport panel provides controls for starting and stopping the session or waveform. Press wind or rewind while playing to scrub forwards or backwards through the file

The view controls allow magnification of any part of the wave or multitrack. Click on autofit to see the whole session.

The selection controls are used in conjunction with the view controls. The size of the selected range is shown here.

The session properties panel contains information about the current session. Tempo and key settings relate to clips which have looping enabled. Use Always Input or Smart Input only with ASIO soundcard drivers installed. Use external monitoring if you are using the Direct X sound driver layer (Audition Windows Sound).

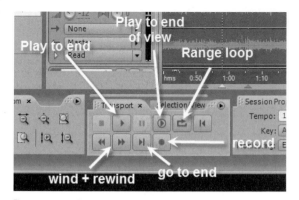

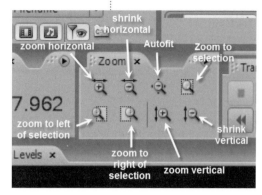

The transport panel.

The view controls.

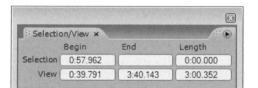

The selection controls.

The session properties.

Panels and tabs are duplicated in the edit view with the exception of the Session Properties panel.

Enabling VST effects in Adobe Audition

VST and Direct X effects need to be set up before Adobe Audition will be able to use them. Adobe Audition does not ship with a default VST directory therefore needs to be told where to find VST effects.

From within the Edit workspace choose Effects, Add / Remove VST Directory from the menu bar. In the VST dialog box browse to the folder containing the VST effects and press OK to add it to the list of locations that Adobe Audition will search for VST effects.

Adobe Audition also supports Direct X effects although this option is not enabled by default. From the effects menu in the edit view choose Enable Direct X Effects. When Direct X effects are enabled you should refresh the effects list to have Adobe Audition scan for new Direct X effects. Close the multitrack view before enabling or refreshing VST or Direct X effects.

VST and Direct X effects need to be set up before Adobe Audition will be able to use them.

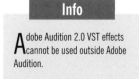

A dobe Audition 2.0 VST effects cannot be used outside Adobe Audition.

Using Adobe Audition

Adobe Audition is a suite of three programs in a single space. All three parts of the program integrate to provide a complete solution from waveform recording to CD production. But all three parts of the program can also be used in isolation when importing waveforms from other programs.

The multitrack view

To see the multitrack view press Shift + F11 or click over the multitrack button on the menu bar.

Provides a workspace for up to 128 Stereo or Mono waveforms and contains a traditional style mixer panel enabling the waveforms to be mixed and balanced in the same way as using traditional analogue mixers. The mixer panel also enables the processing of tracks with real time Adobe effects, VST and Direct X effects and EQ. Complete audio productions may be recorded and produced entirely 'in the box' for exporting to other multi-media programs and devices.

The edit view

To see the edit view press Shift + F10 or click over the edit button on the menu bar.

Enables a single mono or stereo waveform to be played or recorded. In the Edit View the waveform can be analysed processed and shaped using Adobe, VST and Direct X effects. The Edit View is used to create extremely high quality stereo soundtracks, for post production processing, audio preparation and restoration and for scientific analysis and treatments.

The CD view

To see the CD view press Shift + F12 click over the CD button on the menu bar. The CD view is a tool for compiling CD's for distribution. The CD editor produces CD's in 'Red Book' format suitable for pre-mastering. Waveforms created outside Adobe Audition 2.0 can also be used when compiling CD's.

The multitrack view

Within Adobe Audition 2.0, multiple clips can be joined together to produce a complete audio production. The complete production can also include Video or MIDI and the result can be printed to CD from within the program, In Adobe Audition the production is called a session. The multitrack view is where sessions are created. A session is a group of audio, MIDI and video clips arranged along tracks. There are an unlimited number of tracks and each track has EQ and balance properties. Tracks are arranged alongside each other in the mixer panel. Effects and EQ controls are laid out in a familiar format within the mixer. Mixer tracks can also be arranged into busses enabling groups of tracks to be controlled together.

Start Adobe Audition and click the multitrack view button or press Shift + F11 to see the multitrack view.

The default multitrack view is laid out with the folder view on the left, the track panel in the centre left and tracks on the right. Depending on screen

The default multitrack view

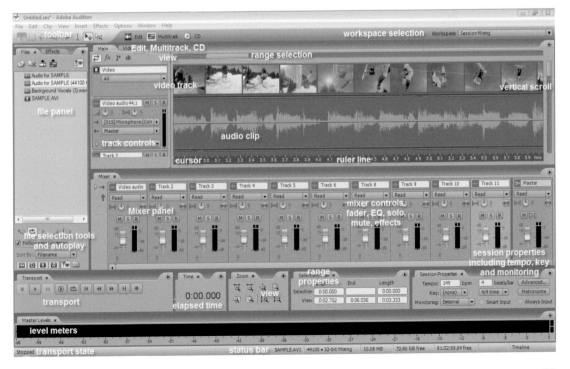

resolution the multitrack view may reveal four or six empty tracks. Further tracks may be revealed if the vertical slider is dragged downwards. Underneath the folder window is the transport panel. The transport panel contains controls for moving forwards and backwards along the tracks. As the session is playing a yellow cursor arranged vertically across all the tracks reveals the current location of the track from beginning to end. The track will play until the yellow cursor reaches the far right of the window after the end of the last clip in the session.

Transport

Adobe Audition uses intuitive VCR style buttons to control playback and location within the track.

Default Transport Shortcuts

| Play and Stop | Spacebar or Alt+P and Alt+S |
| Record | Ctrl+Spacebar |

Left click and hold on either fast forward or fast rewind to scrub along the track. Right click to view scrubbing speed options.

Instant gratification

Adobe Audition is intuitive to use. Little effort is needed to load a waveform and start the track playing.

Find the multitrack view (Shift + F11)
Click over the Import File button in the folder pane and load a cel or waveform. The imported file appears in the folder view
Drag the imported file onto any track
Press the spacebar to start the track
Click over the Mixer tab above track one
Adjust EQ, Balance and effects in the mixer panel.

Understanding clips and waveforms

Waveforms created and saved by almost any program can be imported into Adobe Audition. When an audio file is loaded into Adobe Audition the file is converted into a lossless sample exact format. Adobe Audition encodes the file to the target format when saving.

Any imported waveform becomes a clip. Clips can be moved copied and duplicated around the multitrack session. Clips can contain any sort of audio from speech, to music to scientific recordings and synthesised sounds. Clips may also have properties, such as level EQ or loop properties. A library of prepared clips has been published by Adobe specifically for use in Audition. These clips have preset loop properties making them ideal building blocks for a session.

A new session

Within the multitrack view choose File, New Session from the menu bar. The New Session dialog appears prompting for a sample rate decision. Choose one of the sample rate options. Every waveform recorded or loaded into the session must either be recorded or up/down sampled to match the session frequency rate. The sample rate of the imported file is shown in the section 'Show File Information' on the right of the import dialog. If a file with a different sample rate is imported, a copy of the file will be prepared at the sample rate of the session,

Adobe loops and beds are recorded at 44100 with a 32bit depth; if the new session is based on prepared loops you could choose a new session format of 44100 and avoid having multiple file copies. Bit depth is selected in Adobe Audition multitrack preferences (F4).

Importing prepared files

Audio files must be imported into Audition before they can become clips. Choose Import from the File Menu to produce the import dialogue box and browse to the location of your downloaded file or the file on the CD or other location. To see only see files of a particular type choose from the options in the File Type menu. Adobe Audition 2.0 is able to open almost any audio file format. If you can't see your file type in the selected list choose 'All Files *.*' Adobe Audition will attempt to detect and import the file anyway it can. Click over OK to import the file into the files panel.

Tip

A ny file may be played directly from the open or import dialogue. Click on the file name and choose play from the lower left corner of the dialogue. The Autoplay option causes each file that is selected to be heard without having to press play. Files in any supported format can be played but are not converted to Adobe Audition format so are not downsampled or upsampled. Sometimes this means that files heard in this way will sound different when they are fully imported into the program.

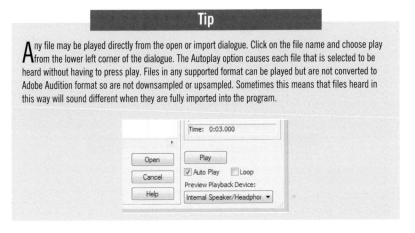

The imported file appears in the files pane on the left of the multitrack view. Autoplay is also supported in the files panel using the options section at the bottom of the panel. If the options section is not displayed use the option button on the top right of the panel to view advanced options.

The advanced options section also contains options for looping the auto-play and a volume control.

If your imported loops have timestretch properties set they will play in this panel at the session tempo. Check the option 'Follow Session Tempo' in this dialogue. Session tempo is set in advanced session properties (Alt +3).

Prepared loops and waveforms are preset to loop rhythmically with no additional processing in Adobe Audition. They are perfect as a basis for a simple session.

After importing the clip, drag from the files panel onto any track in the multitrack view.

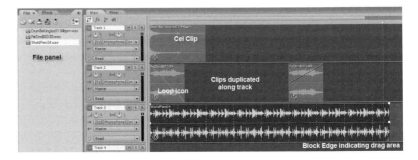

The file will expand to show the contents of the file. The clip can be moved along the track by right-clicking and dragging. Press the spacebar on the computer keyboard. The yellow cursor will move from the far left of the track and as it passes over the loop you should hear the loop play. Press spacebar again to stop.

If you can't hear anything

Look at the level meters at the bottom of the multitrack view. As the cursor moves over the clip the level meters should move. If they don't move it means the track containing the clip is muted. Muted clips appear grey.

Look in Audio Hardware Setup. Click the multitrack tab. Look at the Output section. Ensure that your soundcard driver is loaded. If you have an ASIO driver check the connections and the ASIO control panel. If you are using Audition Windows Sound look in the Direct Sound control panel. Ensure that your preferred device is selected.

Are your headphones or speakers plugged in? If you have a USB or Firewire device check where your headphones are connected. It's possible they are plugged into your laptop rather than the device selected in audio setup.

Repeating the content of the clip is simple. Simply move the mouse to the lower right hand corner of the clip and click and drag along the track. The selected loop will expand along the track and white indicators will appear to show the repeated sections.

The clip will now loop steadily, in time with the session but won't snap to bars unless Snapping is enabled. Snapping will cause clip edges to magnetically stick to the ruler line, to markers or to any number of other options. From the menu bar choose Edit, Snapping and select 'Snap to Ruler (coarse)' and change the ruler display from decimal time to bars and beats by right clicking over the time display panel and choosing 'Bars and Beats' from the list of displayed options. Drag the edge of the clip along the track, the clip edges will now stick to bar and beats in the ruler line and repeat once in every bar.

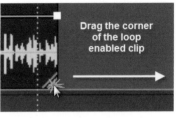

Live Session View

Adding effects to the loop

Effects can be added to the session to introduce interest and to solve simple problems. For instance if you have a voiceover that was recorded in a very dead room you can add some reverb to make the speech easier to listen to.

Click the effects tab in the files panel and click on the small + next to the delay effects section. The effects rack for that track appears. Edit the effect to suit. Compare the dry track with the effected track using the green power button at the bottom of the effects rack. Close the effects rack when finished.

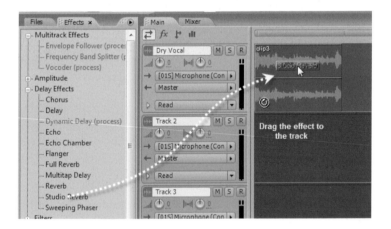

Edit the Studio Reverb effect.

Adding video clips

Now add some more clips. The beauty of prepared loops is that they will always play together and in time. Experiment by loading additional loops into the file panel and dragging them across onto new tracks. A session can have unlimited tracks, dependent on the system on which it is installed. A session can accommodate loops, video and MIDI files. Drag files of each type from the files panel just as with loops. However, there may only be one Video track in each session. Multiple MIDI files can exist in a session.

When a video clip is dragged onto a new track Adobe Audition will export the soundtrack information from the video clip and create a new clip containing the exported soundtrack. This can then be edited and processed just like any other piece of audio.

For instance. If your video soundtrack is too quiet then it can be balanced in the session to make it louder.

1   Drag the video clip into any track and drag to the start of the track
2   Drag the associated audio file onto the next track
3   Click OK
4   Click OK
5   Drag the audio file back to the start of the track
6   Double click the soundtrack waveform. (The waveform will appear loaded into the edit view)
7   Click Effects, Amplitude, Normalize (process)
8   Click OK
9   Press Shift + F11 to return to the multitrack view

The normalize process raises the amplitude of the whole waveform to the point where the loudest part of the waveform is at 100%.

Clips can share tracks and can also be placed on top of each other. The default behaviour of Adobe Audition in this case is to play only the clip lying at the top. This can be changed if you right click over any clip on the track and choose 'Play Hidden Clips' from the menu.

Clip options

While we have the right click menu in mind, let's explore some of the other clip options.

Clips can be cut copied and pasted like any other data. Clips copied in this way are stored on the clipboard and can be pasted anywhere else on the multitrack.

Locking in time prevents the clip from being moved anywhere else on the track although it can still be dragged vertically to another track. This accounts for the biggest difference between Adobe Audition and other DAW programs. That is, Adobe Audition does NOT glue clips into place on the track. Clips are free to move forwards or backwards along the track with a simple right click and drag motion. So, if your production relies on strict time, for instance if you are creating commercial music to a metronome click or along with a sequencer, right click and Lock In time as soon as the new clip is recorded.

Loop properties such as the type of looping and the actions to take inside the session are within the loop properties dialog. If looping is enabled the right click menu will show a tick next to the menu option.

Time stretching is a loop property although it is given its own dialog box. If you want the loop to stretch in time, that is to change pitch rather than tempo if the session temp changes, then choose to enable time stretching here.

Time stretch loops

From the Time Stretch options check Enable Time Stretching and choose Resample (affects pitch). Press OK. The clip will now redraw and will be pitch shifted up or down depending on the difference between the session tempo and the original loop tempo. Return to simple tempo changes by returning to the Time Stretch Property and once again checking 'Enable Time Stretching' then selecting Time Scale Stretch from the drop down menu.

Other clip options

Mute individual clips by choosing Mute from the right click menu. Splitting loops is a non-destructive way to quickly tidy up your session. Loops and clips can easily be trimmed to length without destroying or even changing the contents of the clip. The loop or clip is split at the position of the yellow cursor.

Moving clips

By now you should have a pretty good idea that clips are powerful objects which can be copied, split and changed anywhere inside your production. But your session wouldn't be very useful if all you could do was play clips from the start of the track. Clips must be selected before they can be moved.

Select any clip by left clicking once inside the clip. Selected clips turn dark green. Now with the right mouse button, click and drag the selected clip anywhere else inside the session, even to another track.

Mouse actions in the edit view

Left click	Selects clip
Right click and hold	Produces clip menu
Left click and drag	Range select
Right click and drag	Move clip
Shift and right click and drag	Mirrors clip
Ctl and right click and drag	Duplicates (makes a new waveform from clip)
Left click and drag right edge of clip	Block edge dragging (loop repeats)

Move Copy Clip tool

A convenient way to move or copy clips is provided in the form of the Move Copy tool. This is found on the upper left corner of the default multitrack view. Click on the tool to select it and use the tool to pick up any clip and move it within the session. If the right mouse button is used Adobe Audition will present the following options:

Copy Reference here	A reference copy of the clip is created. Changes made to the source waveform will affect all referenced copies
Copy Unique here	A unique copy (clone) of the source waveform is created at the position in the session. Changes to the source waveform will not affect unique copies.
Move Clip here	The clip is simply moved to the new location.

All of these actions are duplicated in the various shift+drag or ctrl+drag combinations.

Save the new session by choosing File, Save Session from the File menu.

Zoom in and out

With more than a few clips in your multitrack session you may find that the window is no longer large enough for all the clips in the session to be seen at once. Use the tools available in the Zoom panel to zoom in and out of the session. Alternatively click and drag one side of the horizontal range bar above the session to shrink or expand the current view.

Click and drag the range bar to extend the view.

Live Session View

Balancing the track volumes

Clips play just fine by themselves. But some of the clips may need to be balanced. Track volume controls are placed to the left of each track within the main panel. Depending on the size of the main panel the volume controls maybe hidden. Position the mouse cursor in the small space between adjoining tracks. When you see the drag tool click and drag the lower edge of the track downwards, Volume and pan rotary controls are placed just under the track name.

Track properties

Use the rotary controls to change overall volume and pan for each track. The Mute control button (M) can also be used to mute the entire track if necessary. Likewise the Solo control (S) will mute all tracks except the solo'd track.

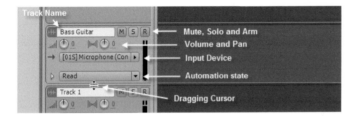

Group waveform normalize

Waveforms recorded at different times may have different amplitudes. This is a problem when using multiple clips in a session as levels may vary from track to track and even from clip to clip within the track. Group normalizing examines the amplitudes inside waveforms used in the session and balances the waveform amplitudes of the group.

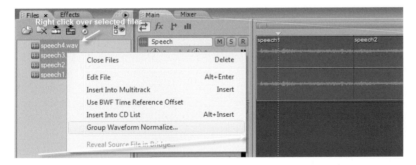

Normalizing a waveform means to raise the level of each sample in the waveform by the difference between the loudest sample and 0dBfs. A normalized waveform is at the maximum level allowed by the content of the waveform without affecting the dynamics of the audio.

1 Click select or shift select clips in the files panel
2 Use the analyse tool if necessary to see the results of the normalize procedure in figures.
3 Choose the normalize options. When all the waveforms are to be used in

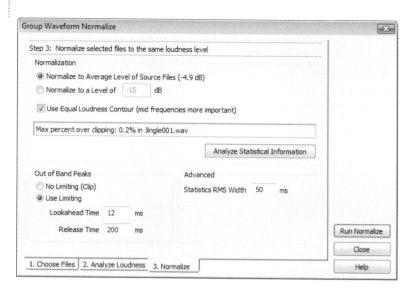

the session the option to average the waveforms will produce the best results. If the waveforms are to be used in the edit view, the option to normalize without the average can be used instead.

Group waveform normalizing is a destructive process which may change the sound of the audio. If the waveforms are closed when the session is closed the original waveform will be destroyed as changes are written to the original. Open each waveform in the edit view and use the Save Copy As feature to make a copy of the original file before normalizing.

Snapping

Loops or other rhythmic clips need to be placed carefully in the session. If clips are placed behind or ahead of the beat the loop will appear to be out of time. To make dropping clips into the right place easier, Adobe Audition has a snapping feature. Various snapping options enable clips to be placed accurately within the session.

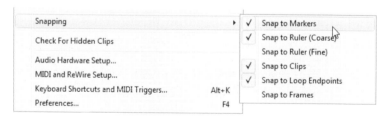

Edit, snapping

Each of the snap options is independent and can be turned off or used in combination with other options.

Snap to Rulers causes clips to snap magnetically to the closest ruler increment. Choose Snap To Ruler (Fine) then right click and drag a clip forward or backward in the track to the nearest bar. Adobe Audition does not have grid-

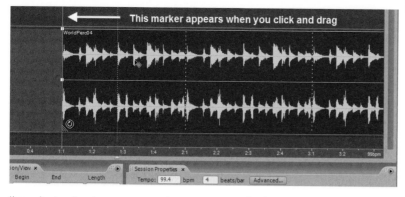

lines. Instead, a temporary marker appears at the leading edge of the clip as you drag. Drag the clip until the lower edge of the marker is at the desired point on the ruler line.

Clips can also be set to snap to other clips, to markers, to loop endpoints or to frames. Depending on the arrangement these options may be useful or not. For instance, when creating commercial music the snap to ruler option is essential as clips must be placed strictly in time. On the other hand if creating a video or film soundtrack the snap to markers option is relevant and snapping to the ruler may be disabled if unused.

Snap to ruler has two modes; coarse and fine. Coarse will cause the ruler to snap to major ruler increments only. Snapping to Ruler (fine) causes the clip to stick to minor increments. Snapping is enabled for any display time format; Bars and Beats, Decimal, Frames, etc.

Session properties

Tempo

Loops and prepared waveforms are usually arranged in folders grouped by tempo. Creating a meaningful piece of soundtrack music is therefore simple as it is a simple job to load clips with the same tempo into your session. The session tempo will change to the tempo of the first loop that is dragged onto a track. All subsequent loops will inherit the same tempo. However the session tempo may not be exactly what you need. In this case you must edit the session tempo, part of session properties.

Adjust tempo by overtyping the new tempo in the tempo field and then pressing enter on the keyboard. The session will redraw to accommodate the new tempo. If the loaded clips have timestretch properties you may adjust the key of the session (relative to the keys of the loaded clips) using the Key drop down menu. The time signature field does not affect the time signature of loaded clips. Changing the time signature will simply change the increments on the ruler line and the metronome beat, the clips will remain unaffected.

Tip

Press and hold Ctrl when dragging any clip to temporarily defeat snapping.

Advanced session properties

Clicking over the Advanced button in the Session Properties panel produces the Advanced Session Properties window. This has five tabs. For this session, we'll look at the tempo and metronome tabs.

The tempo tab contains controls found on the main panel with the addition of a 'ticks / beat' control and an offset control. Offset is the difference between the true beginning of the session and another point, further along the session. For example; you may wish your session to start after the 'true' beginning because of a video countdown. The offset control enables you to reset the start of the session to the current position of the cursor.

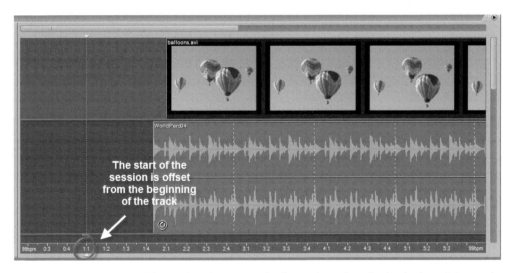

The start of the session is offset from the beginning of the track

In this session the start point is one bar after the beginning of the track. This is to allow for a count to be inserted before the start point.

Metronome

The metronome provides a way to mark bars and beats as the track plays. Musicians are familiar with using the metronome to keep time and Adobe Audition has a useful metronome feature.

The metronome sound can be changed to suit and the metronome volume adjusted in decibels. Use minus figures to lower the metronome volume or assign the metronome to it's own set of outputs. Turn the metronome on or

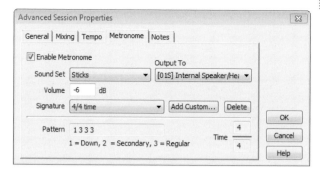

off from within the Session Properties panel or assign a shortcut key within the Keyboard Shortcuts and MIDI Triggers options dialog. (Edit, Keyboard Shortcuts and MIDI Triggers).

Exporting the session into other programs

The collection of balanced and arranged loops in your session can now be exported and used in any other multimedia application. The simplest way to export your session is to simply render the session as you hear it into an mp3 file.

Exporting your session as an mp3

Arrange the session exactly as you want it to be heard including any muted or balanced tracks. From the file menu choose Export, Mixdown.

1   From within the Export Audio window choose the options for your mixdown. An mp3 file is smaller than a wave and good if the audio is non-critical, for use in a mobile presentation etc,

2   Choose 'master as the source. The master is the audio heard from the headphone output or single pair of stereo outputs. If your soundcard has

multiple outputs the master source is the combination of all the output pairs combined.

3 Dither your file to 16 bit

4 Name your file and set all the options. Click on the save button to produce the exported session as a single stereo mp3. The mp3 will automatically be loaded into the edit view for additional editing if necessary.

Notes; Uncompressed audio saved as .wav files are the highest quality. However they are also the largest files. Save audio intended for an iPod in mp3 format and import into iTunes in the usual way;

1 In Edit view, press Ctrl+P to invoke the file properties dialog.

2 Choose the Text Fields tab and choose MP3 (ID tag) from the drop down menu.

3 Enter track details in these fields for display on the iPod.

Exporting a combined audio and video session

A session containing a Video track may be exported as a new video file. In this way a video containing a new soundtrack may be created from a Adobe Audition 2.0 session. The video may be saved under a different name. Choose File, Export, Video to start the process. The video export process has just a single step. Accept the defaults and press OK to start the export.

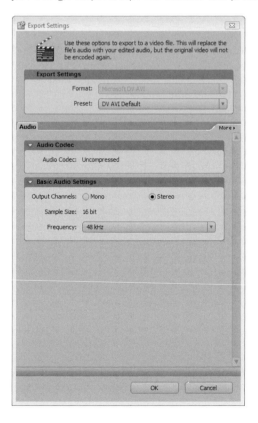

XMP information

XMP is the Adobe Extensible Metadata Platform. Files containing XMP can carry additional information tags along with the video. In this way copyright and IPR details along with index information can be associated permanently with the file when it is created. The encoded data can be used by XMP compatible operating systems and devices. XMP information can be attached to video files exported from Adobe Audition. Click on the 'More' link just above the audio properties to see the XMP details window.

Next step; recording waves to be used in a session, mixing and arrangement

A simple session can be created using pre-programmed loops. These sessions don't have to be complex and are perfect for video soundtracks or beds, or as background music. However recording audio isn't complex and with a little practice your own waveforms and loops will be more valuable than anything you can download.

Create a new session

If necessary, close the current session. Choose File, Save Session from the Menu bar. When a session is closed the files from the session remain in the file panel for use in any further session. If necessary close these files and clear the panel entirely by choosing File, Close Unused Media from the menu bar.

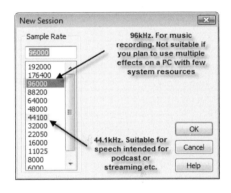

From the file menu choose New Session. Adobe Audition will prompt you for a decision regarding the sample rate for the new session. Sample rate is the speed at which Adobe Audition will record data. Choose a sample rate appropriate to the session. A session intended for a film soundtrack requires a high sample rate and bit depth. A session for a podcast needs a lower sample rate and bit depth.

Sample rate and bit depth

Generally high sample rates are preferable. Your recordings and processes will be high quality and low sample rate exported audio will benefit from the high quality source.

Choose a minimum sample rate of 44100 kHz. Choose 96000 if your soundcard will support it. Bit depth (16 bit or 32 bit) is decided in the Multitrack preferences. Spatial effects such as reverb produce a high quality result in 32bits but at the expense of performance.

Bit depth

Bit depth is the number of bits in the sample. A bit is a binary number. Larger numbers enable a greater range of information to be stored about the sample. This translates into a higher quality recording.

A waveform containing 44.1 thousand samples per second tells the computer that 'something' happened 44.1 thousand times each second in the course of the recording. Smaller bit depth doesn't give the computer much of an idea about what happened. Greater bit depth enables the computer to know more about what happened and so in turn is able to reproduce a better audio reproduction of the events in that recording.

Musicians and technicians talk in terms of '24/96' or '24/48'. These numbers are shorthand for bit depth and sample rate. For example 24/96 means; '96000, 24 bit samples per second'.

Don't be blinded into thinking that larger numbers are always better. Digital data must always be converted down to lower rate/sample format for use in everything from digital radio to podcasts. This conversion is called 'downsampling'. During this process, Adobe Audition must examine the data and apply mathematical algorithms to it. The nature of these algorithms and their effect on the recording can very dramatically depending on source format of the waveform, the intended target format and the nature of the material that was recorded.

During downsampling Adobe Audition takes the high resolution waveform and makes a lower resolution copy of it. To do this it must literally 'lose' data. This data loss must be as invisible as possible so a process called 'dithering' is applied to the data. Dithering masks the new holes in the data with tiny amounts of digital noise. The amount and type of noise created changes depending on the type of dithering applied. Higher bit depth means much more dithering, or more noise. This noise isn't apparent in the down sampled waveform but it is artificial and does affect the sound of your mix.

Audio preferences and monitoring

Adobe Audition needs to be told which device your mixer or instrument is connected to. The default input device then becomes the first input device in the track controls.

Find Audio Hardware preferences (Edit, Audio Hardware Setup). In the Multitrack tab choose the ASIO driver for your soundcard or the Audition Windows Sound driver if the soundcard does not have an ASIO driver. At the bottom of the Multitrack tab there is a drop down menu for Input and Output devices. Choose the default input and default output devices for your session. Every track will inherit these defaults which will save you time when working through your session. Press OK to save your preferences.

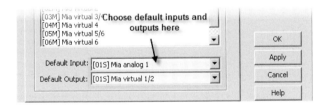

Monitoring

Adobe Audition provides a choice of monitoring options:

External

External monitoring relies on an external device to route audio from the incoming device to headphones or speakers. Another pair of connections is then used to send audio to the input of the soundcard and back to the mixer. Typically an external mixer is used in this configuration. When external monitoring is used Adobe Audition cannot reproduce the input audio at the output device. The only way audio can be reproduced is if Adobe Audition is playing back a waveform. The external option is provided for low powered systems or older soundcards with high latency. If you consistently hear long delays between incoming and outgoing signals, or if audio disappears periodically, choose the external monitor option. This is the option with the lowest load on your processor.

Audition mix

When Audition Mix monitoring is selected audio will be routed from the input device to the output device without the need for external devices. This produces a very flexible environment as control remains within Adobe Audition. In addition VST effects such as reverb can be used on source material. This in turn opens up the possibility of using things such as VST filtering or distortion effects on instruments. In this way Audition Mix enables Adobe Audition to become an external effects processor for your keyboards, guitars and other devices.

Audition mix monitoring options

Smart input. Input is heard only when a track is armed for record. Input is not heard when playing back. Instead, clips on the armed track are played. This is closest to the traditional function of a recording device.

Always input. Input is monitored in record and play. In addition clips on the armed track are not played back. Instead the input sound is heard.

Using VST effects while recording

Provided that the PC is provided with enough resources, VST effects can be used to process any signal in real time. A performance PC with a low latency soundcard can be used as a very high powered effects processor, a guitar amp or a set of DJ decks.

Testing levels into the multitrack

Connect a recording device to the input of your soundcard. Press F10 on the computer keyboard to test levels. If this is the first waveform for the untitled session Adobe Audition will prompt for a name for the session. Waveforms will be saved in a folder underneath the folder in which the session is stored. So if the session is called 'c:\test.ses' a folder called 'c:\test_recorded' will be created to store the waveforms created in the session. Adobe Audition does not prompt to store waveforms. Every recording created in the session is stored automatically.

When the file is named and stored Adobe Audition will return you to the multitrack view. Depending on your soundcard settings you may need to set monitoring up within Adobe Audition in order to hear the incoming audio.

In External monitoring mode. With the instrument or other sound source connected to the soundcard press F10 on the keyboard. The level meters should move, indicating that Adobe Audition is receiving audio.

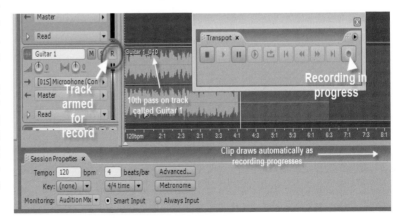

In Audition Mix mode. Record arm any track. The source input will appear at the output.

Recording levels

Digital levels are always referred to in minus numbers relative to 0dBfs (zero decibels full scale). Optimum level depends on the sample rate and the nature of your sound card. Aim to have peaks at no more that -8db. This allows headroom for very fast peaks known as transients, and also provides room for calculations required when downsampling. Right click ove the level meters to adjust the dynamic range view of the meters

Recording with guitar effects

Real time recording of guitar effects or other real time effects is only possible when Adobe Audition is used in Audition Mix mode. Audition Mix routes the input source through the effects rack during recording but doesn't record the effects.

1 Connect the guitar to the external mixer or soundcard and make connections to route the sound of the guitar directly through the computer, not as a sidechain or auxiliary.
2 In Session Properties at the lower right of the screen, choose Audition Mix as the monitoring type. Alternatively choose Monitoring, Audition Mix, Smart Input from the Options menu.
3 Press the record enable button to the left of the track and check that levels are good without clipping. The level meters should rise and fall with your playing
4 Disable the track record and select the Track Properties 'FX' view using the toggles above the track properties. An empty effects rack will appear in the track properties.
5 Click on the 'twisty' triangle to the left of one of the effects slots to see the effects menu and populate the effect rack with effects.
6 Record enable the track again to hear the effects.

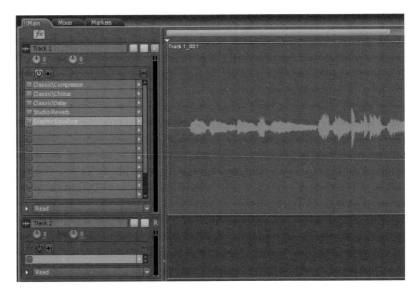

Press the record button on the play bar when you want to start recording. Play the track back and power the effects rack off to hear the difference between the recorded sound and the recorded sound with effects.

When you are happy with effects, freeze the track in the mixer panel to conserve resources. If you want to permanently tie the track in with the effects mixdown the track (right click in any track and Export to File) and import the mixdown back into the session.

Recording the first waveform

Arm the first track in the session with the red R button in the track controls. If the session has not been named you will be prompted for a name for the session and a location for the recorded wave files. If the session properties have not yet been set you will be prompted to set a sampling rate for the session.

Play something on the guitar or microphone etc. attached to the soundcard input. The level meters on the armed track should move to illustrate the level detected by Audition. If the level meters don't move you should check the following;

1 That your soundcard is detected in Audio Hardware Preferences.
2 That the correct input channel is selected in the armed track.
3 That Audition Mix is selected as the monitoring type in session properties. (note Audition Mix requires a low latency ASIO soundcard. If external monitoring is selected you will not see any input levels until the new waveform is drawn as the transport is moving.

If your audio is to be set to strict time, you may need to start the metronome. Press Alt+3 to see session properties if not already visible. Click over the metronome button to hear the metronome in play and record. If the metronome is not heard check the metronome output in Advanced Session Properties.

Get ready to perform or produce some audio and use the mouse to press the red record button on the transport (keyboard shortcut; Ctrl+Spacebar).

During the recording the cursor line will move across the screen and the waveform will be drawn in the track behind if. When the cursor reaches the far right of the screen Adobe Audition will scroll to enable the new waveform to be displayed as it is drawn. Press Spacebar again to stop recording. The newly recorded waveblock appears on

Tip

The effects may temporarily be disabled when leaving the effects rack after editing effects. if this happens re-arm the track for record to hear the effects again in realtime.

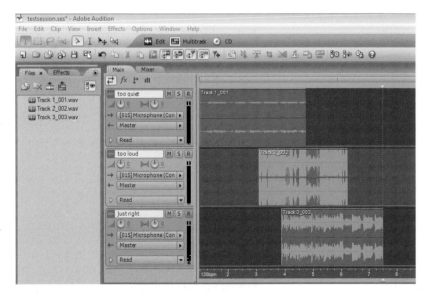

the track and is named and saved automatically. Adobe Audition does not require you to save waveblocks individually.

Adobe Audition will record for as long as you wish within certain limits. The maximum file size for am Adobe Audition recording is 4GB. Depending on your session properties this may give you a single stereo recording length of around 9 hours at 32Bits 44100kHz. Divide this figure by the number of tracks that you have to record. For instance if you have an eight input sound-card and wish to record 4 stereo pairs you may see a maximum session length of about two hours.

Watch your recording levels very carefully. In this first session there are three new recorded waveforms. The first is recorded too quietly and will need additional processing to raise the volume of the waveform. Raising the volume also raises any noise in the waveform and so should be avoided if possible. The second waveform has been recorded with too much level. The waveform is shown hard up against the top of the clip indicating that clipping is taking place. This waveform won't ever be useful as clipping introduces distortion which can't be removed. This recording must be redone. The third recording is 'just right'. The waveform peaks at about two thirds of the space inside the clip and leaves plenty of headroom for peaks and transients.

Multiple tracks may be recorded at a time. If you use a soundcard or firewire device with multiple in and outputs, these can be assigned to different tracks. Press Shift and Ctrl when selecting input and out put devices to copy that assignment to all tracks in the session.

Recorded levels

Adobe Audition 2.0 contains no controls to raise or lower the amount of level coming into the record track. Raising or lowering the track fader in the mixer panel has an effect on the output of the recording but not on the input. If you track is too quiet or too loud you must use the level controls on the external mixer or the soundcard controls to affect how much level is received by Adobe Audition.

Track properties

To the left of each track are track properties. Depending on the current view and zoom (including the resolution of your monitor) some of these options may not be visible. Select the required set of controls from the toggles at the top of the track properties panel.

Tip

Move any track up or down the multitrack view simply by clicking and dragging the icon next to the track name. The new arrangement is reflected in the mixer panel too.

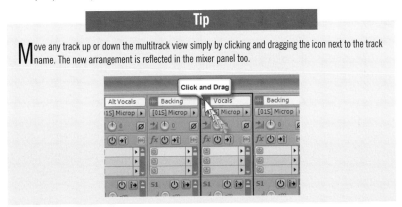

Putting clips to work

Clips are the building blocks of your session. A clip is a child of a waveform. Changes to the clip are not made to the parent and numerous clips can be made from the same waveform. Importantly, clips are tiny in size compared to the waveform but can be duplicated over and over. This means that the session takes far less disk space than a session in which multiple unique copies of the waveform are created and used.

Making a rhythm track from a short stereo drum sample

Stereo drum tracks are everywhere on the net. Find a short rhythmic section with a steady beat. It's a paradox but the parts that 'feel' the best are often the parts that don't work well when cut and pasted together. That's because it's the human feel of the track that is producing the swing we like to hear.

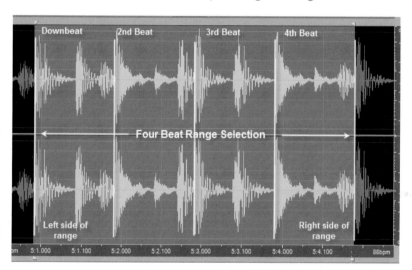

Live Session View

Open the drum track in the edit view and carefully find and mark four or eight beat ranges in the stereo waveform. Create a range by dragging over the waveform. A little trial and error is required in identifying the beats in the waveform. It's easiest to identify the downbeat first and drag a short selection on from that. Create shortcut keys for Edit, Adjust Selection (Left Side, Left and Right – Right Side, Left and Right) and use these keyboard shortcuts to shrink and expand the range. This is easier than using the mouse as a new mouse click will change the start of the range – which needs to be set exactly. When auditioning the range, use the loop play option. It's much easier to hear how the range works in a loop.

With the range set exactly as you wish, press the F8 button on the keyboard. Range makers are created around the range and an entry is added to the Marker List. Create ranges for Intro, Fills, Clicks etc.

View the marker list (Alt+8) to see the ranges in a list. Use the label field to name each range. You can also autoplay from the marker list. Double click an entry in the list to go to that entry in the waveform. You'll now see that a small + has been added to the filename in the file panel. This indicates that markers have been created in the file. If you can't see the + sign use 'Show

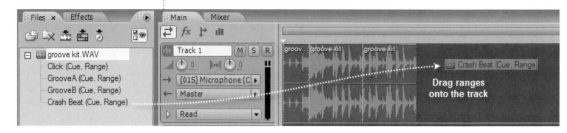

Markers' in the options section at the bottom of the files panel. When markers have been renamed, save the file.

Ranges in the clip can now be used as clips in the multitrack view. Switch to the multitrack view. Because you have recorded the file in Adobe Audition the waveform is already imported into the files panel as a clip. Expand the clip to show clip ranges. Drag ranges from the file panel onto the multitrack view in any order.

A complete drum track can be made using only the ranges created in the edit view. The new track can be any length. No matter how long the track, the source waveform will never change size.

Zero crossings

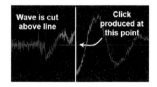

A zero crossing is a point in the waveform where the amplitude of the wave is near enough Zero. Using these Zero crossings when finding loop start and end points means that you can avoid the pops and clicks that occur when a range bisects a wave at a point above or below the zero amplitude line. Find Zero Crossings on the Edit menu in the edit view.

1 Drag select a range just over the loop length
2 With the range selected choose 'Find Zero Crossings' in the Edit menu
3 Use the shortcut keys to shift the edges of the range in and out until a seamless loop with no clicks can be heard.

The Zero Crossings feature is also useful when creating multisampled string or piano loops, and when cutting vocal phrases.

Creating simple drum loops

The new drum track works great. However if you drag the edge of any clip you'll find that the clip extends to reveal the source waveform. The clip doesn't loop because loop properties for each clip aren't yet set. Before the loop can be created we must discover the tempo of the original waveform and use that in our session.

Double click on any clip to open the clip in the edit view. The view range is automatically set to the clip. Check that Snap to Markers is enabled and drag select over the range between the blue range markers at the extreme right and left edge of the range.

1 Right click over the time display panel and choose Edit Tempo from the right click menu. Enter the number of beats in the range and choose Extract. Adobe Audition will analyse the range and calculate the tempo.

Note the displayed tempo, press OK and return to the multitrack view.

2 Enter the new tempo in the session properties panel.

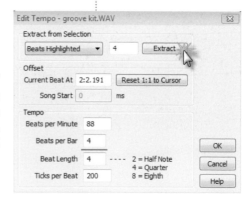

Now the session tempo is correct with the base tempo of the source waveform, we can continue to create loops from the clips. To enable matching tempo to session tempo the loop properties of the source waveform have to be set. A new waveform with individual properties must be created from each clip.

1 In the multitrack view right click over a clip and choose convert to unique copy from the menu. The name of the clip is changed and another clip appears in the file panel.

2 Double click over the clip to open in edit view

3 From the File Menu choose File Info and choose the Loop Info tab from the File Info dialogue. Choose One Shot loops and check that the number of beats is the number of beats in the range. Press OK.

4 Choose Save As from the File menu. Give the new loop clip a meaningful name and save the file, ensuring that non-audio information is also saved.

5 Return to the multitrack view and right click over the newly created and saved clip. Choose Loop Properties from the menu.

6 Enable looping to repeat at the same frequency (four beats) as the source clip. Press OK

A loop indicator appears on the clip. Drag edges of the clip to produce the loop. Enable Snapping to Ruler (coarse) to enable simple matching of the loop to the ruler.

Inserting new tracks within the session

Sessions are created from numerous waveform files. Clips are edited parts of these files distributed around the session. Clips are non destructive. Deleting a clip does not delete the file. Clips can also have their own properties. A

duplicated clip may exist many times, on separate tracks, with different volume and pan attributes and different effects. Loops may be created from clips without changing the source waveform.

My session has a number of elements including clips, loops and whole waveforms. So far I've filled the six default tracks with loops and some recorded waveforms. I've added a vocal part to track six but now I need to add additional backing vocals. To do this I need to insert an audio track.

To insert a new audio track use Insert, Audio Track from the menu bar. Alternatively use the keyboard shortcut Alt+A. The new Audio Track is placed at the bottom of the track panel. This is new track number 7.

The backing vocal take is recorded onto track 7 and all my recorded tracks are now locked in time to avoid mistakes made by accidentally moving the clip when producing the right click menu.

Editing and dropping (punching) in
Performers make all sorts of mistakes when recording music and speech and so the option to edit and correct recordings is vital in any system designed for recording from an imperfect source such as humans!

Editing
Parts of the wave block may need correcting. There are two approaches to this.

If the 'wrong' part is at the beginning or end of the performance and there is a large gap between phrases you may lock the entire waveform in time and manually split the waveform around the incorrect part.

To lock and split a clip;

1 Right click over the clip and choose 'Lock In Time'
2 Split the clip by left clicking once inside the clip.
3 Place the position marker (yellow cursor) at the required place on the clip and press Ctrl+K.

The clip is now split. Delete the incorrect part and set the yellow cursor in front of the part to be recorded. Record a new part and stop the transport before the yellow cursor reaches the next good phrase. This will leave your first recording intact and create a second recording on the same track.

If there is no usable gap between phrases you may need to 'Punch In'.

Punch in

The punch in feature enables a recording range to be set over just a portion of any clip on the track. This is a non destructive act; numerous passes can be made by the performer. Passes are reviewed later and the best one chosen

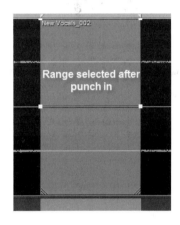

Range selected after punch in

1 Mark the punch in and out points by pressing F8 at the beginning and end of phrase or section that needs attention. Marker points will appear over the multitrack view.
2 If necessary use Edit, Snapping, Snap to Markers to make selecting the range easier and zoom in on the selected range.
3 Select the clip and use the time select tool or drag select the section between the markers.
4 Right click over the selection and choose Punch In from the right click menu

The record range is now set. If necessary right click over the record button on the transport and choose the Loop Recording option. Adobe Audition will cycle around the recording and make as many passes as necessary. Loop recording is indicated by the record button icon. Loop recording is only possible if the track marker is set at the start of the record range. If the track marker is set behind the track range, loop recording will not happen even though loop recording has been selected. If loop recording is not necessary simply set the position marker ahead of the record range and use the normal record option,

5 Make as many passes as necessary and stop recording. The passes are displayed in the file panel.

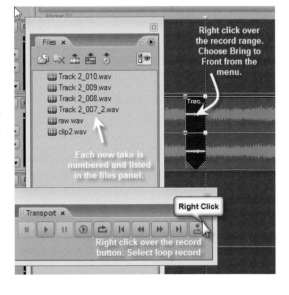

Right click over the record range. Choose Bring to Front from the menu.

Each new take is numbered and listed in the files panel.

Right Click

Right click over the record button. Select loop record

6 Right click over the recorded range and choose Bring To Front from the menu. Each pass is displayed.
7 Choose and listen to each pass in turn, when you have found the one to keep right click over the clip and deselect Punch In.

The new punch in clip is loosely joined to the underlying clip. If the underlying clip is moved, the punch in clip will move with it. However, the punch in clip can also be moved off the underlying clip. Sometimes creating a complex performance with frequent corrections can take a significant amount of time. When the track is complete, right click over the track and bounce the entire track to a new track as a complete waveform.

It's not possible to punch into a loop enabled clip.

Managing files

To the left of the track controls is the files panel. Recorded files are automatically named and added to the list of files in the session. Files take the name of the track and numbered sequentially in the whole session. All the files in the session are named in the panel along with files or loops, etc. that you may have opened but not used in the session. This list can get very long. To remove unused files use File, Close Unused Media from the menu bar.

During the recording other clips can be dragged and moved around the session and effects and other processes can be changed for other tracks.

Tip

Lock the new waveform in time immediately after recording. It's easy to move clips out of time when looking for the right click menu. The best way to do this is not to use the right click menu but to create a keyboard shortcut which can be toggled when the recording is finished. Choose Edit, Lock In Time from the list of available multitrack commands and assign any unused key (such as L).

Removing waveforms completely

Adobe Audition saves each waveform as you record. However you may be certain that the recording is completely wrong and will never need to be recalled. In this case click on the newly created waveblock and press Shift + Backspace. Adobe Audition will warn you that the waveblock is in the session. Accept the warning. The waveblock is destroyed permanently. Be careful. Waves are removed completely including all edit levels and are not sent to the recycle bin. Alternatively click and delete an unused waveblock to remove from the session but not from the file store.

Audio File Cleanup

Adobe Audition saves each take automatically. This is by design, previous versions of Adobe Audition required the user to make a decision regarding the future of each waveform as soon as it had been recorded, seriously interrupting the workflow of a session. During an Adobe Audition 2.0 session many hundreds of files can be created (depending on the performance of your talent of course). Of these only a small number will ever be used, the rest will contain false starts, coughs and other interruptions. Unless you are planning a gag reel these will never be used and will take up space.

Edward Hamlin has created a useful utility for Adobe Audition 2.0 which will remove unused waveforms permanently from the computer.

- Download Audio File Cleanup from http://www.edwardhamlin.com/afc_download.shtml
- Save the session and leave Adobe Audition running in the background.
- Start Audio File Cleanup. The program will detect the session and the location of the session files then will determine how many files exist in the session folder but are not used in the current arrangement. These are then shown as white in the files list
- Decide if you want to move or delete the files. You can even print a list of the unused files for later.

Arranging waveforms and clips within the session

Remove recorded clips by selecting the clip and pressing the delete key on the keyboard. This action simply removes the clip from the session but the file from which the clip is created, and any other clips created from that file are not removed. Alternatively destroy the clip completely by selecting the clip. Holding the shift key down and pressing the delete key. This closes the file associated with the clip and deletes all clips created from that file from the computer and is not recoverable.

To select multiple clips; select the first clip then hold the ctrl key while selecting subsequent clips.

Splitting, trimming and duplicating clips

The backing vocal waveform has some background noise which we need to remove. Because our session is using snapping to ruler, we can create useful blocks of backing vocals which can be copied around the session.

Right click over the time panel and choose bars and beats from the list of options. Find the bar line just before the start of the backing vocals and click inside the clip to place the yellow cursor on the beat.

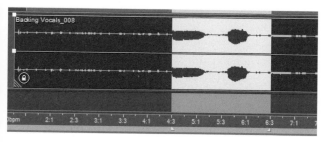 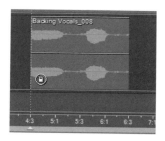

Hold the left button down while moving the mouse to create an eight beat range. The cursor will snap to the bar line for accuracy. With the range selected, right click over the range and select trim (Ctrl+T) from the menu. The area outside the selected range will be removed leaving just the backing vocal selection (above right).

Duplicate this clip to other parts of the song using the move/copy clip tool.

Alternatively shift click and drag a duplicate across the session. Duplicated clips are renamed with a suffix indicating the number of duplications created from the clip. Eg; Backing Vocals_008 (2)

If the source clip is locked in time, duplicates will also be locked in time. In this case, duplicate clips are created and laid on top of the source clip. This is confusing as it appears as though no clip has been created. The file panel will show the newly created clip with the new duplicate clip number. Alternatively unlock the clip and move along the track. There are times when you may not wish to experiment by moving a clip to see if one is underneath, particularly when involved in a complex session with sample accurate requirements. In this case drag the locked clip vertically or downwards to a new track. If the clip is a duplicate you will see the source clip in place. On the other hand if you have mistakenly dragged the source clip, it is only a matter of safely dragging to back to the correct channel.

Because the session is snapping to the ruler it is easy to move duplicated clips into place with some accuracy. This is particularly useful when creating western or pop music as most sections need only to be four or eight bars in length and need to be moved eight or sixteen bars. When creating music like this it is simple to record or import just a handful of clips and move them into place along the ruler.

Editing speech or classical music is more difficult as edit points may not be always on the bar, In these cases, place the cursor carefully between bars or remove snapping completely (Edit, Snapping) Trimming and splitting clips is entirely non-destructive. The trimmed region can be expanded to recover any hidden information at any time. Simply drag either end of the trimmed clip.

Clip length can also be trimmed to remove noise or unwanted parts. Trim clip length by dragging either end of the clip. Clips may also be split in the same way as they are trimmed. Click on the point of the waveform that you wish the clip to be split at, and choose Split from the right click menu.

Merging and muting

Clips can be merged, but only if they share the same source waveform. To merge two clips select one of the parts and right click, choose merge. The clips need to be touching and no parts missing from between the sections to be joined.

Clips can also be muted completely. Simply right click over the clip and choose mute from the right click menu. The muted clip is dark grey and multiple clips may be selected and muted.

Grouping and arranging clips

A waveform that has been split into smaller sections may still need to be moved as one part. For example the vocal track in this session has been split to remove unwanted noise between verses. However if we were to move one of the clips the others would remain in place possibly leading to problems in timing. The solution to this is to group non contiguous clips together. Grouped clips can then be moved, deleted etc. as one.

Group clips by selecting multiple clips (ctrl+click over each clip). Right click over one of the selected clips and choose Group Clips from the menu. The clips are now in a group and can be moved together.

Grouped clips can also be duplicated in one action. This allows multiple tracks to be created from one set of grouped clips. For example, the Backing Vocal parts in this session have been duplicated to another track where they'll be processed with additional delay to produce the effect of a large choir from just one backing vocal.

Clip properties

Clip properties for volume and pan are applied before envelopes. Envelopes are applied to the relative level of the clip as set in the clip property. To find clip properties, right click over any clip and choose Clip Properties from the menu. Alternatively press Ctrl + H with any clip selected.

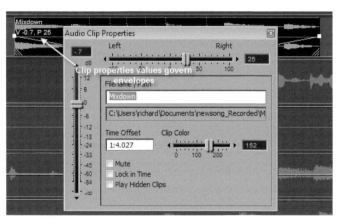

Alongside volume and pan properties are additional controls for colour and also for naming the clip. Volume and pan values from Clip Properties are displayed within each clip as soon as the value is changed from the default of 0db and centre (0).

Envelopes

By now the waveform is full with duplicated clips and loops. The sound of this session is pretty chaotic. Every clip is playing at the level it was recorded and most of the clips are monaural (both sides of the stereo image are identical). So it's a boring, noisy mono mix which needs some cheering up.

Simple and complex changes in balance (volume) and pan are easy to cre-

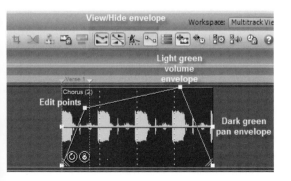

Tip

Panning a clip hard right in Clip Properties will cause Adobe Audition 2.0 to halt (crash) without warning. This is a known bug in version 2.0. Use envelopes or track properties to manage the pan effect.

ate using the envelope feature. Envelopes are changes to clip properties which are drawn onto the clip itself. Along with volume and pan, envelopes can be created for effect parameters. A new feature in Adobe Audition 2.0 is the ability to change MIDI tempo using envelopes. This becomes very useful, particularly when matching a piece of music to a video clip, or even for slow 'rallentando' fades. MIDI tempo envelopes are drawn directly onto the clip, in exactly the same way as volume or pan envelopes. View, Show MIDI Tempo Envelopes.

Envelopes are non-destructive and can be completely different from clip to clip, even if the clips are duplicated. Envelopes are copied if the clip is duplicated or cloned but not if the clip is applied to a looped section which is then expanded. Make envelope changes to the loop then duplicate the loop to make a four or eight bar section. Then group the duplicated clips (complete with envelopes) to make a block which can then be duplicated along the session. Duplicated and cloned clips are always orphaned, in other words they no longer have a relationship with the source clip or waveform (other than if the source waveform is destroyed, the clips are also destroyed). Envelope changes in the source clip will not be reflected in duplicated clips.

Envelope power is relative to the clip property. If the clip level in the clip property is -3db, the envelope power can never exceed that same level. If the pan control is set to one side, the centre line of the clip will be at that same value – but the pan envelope will still appear to be central.

Envelopes are used when you need to change the nature of a clip, before that clip becomes useful in the mix. Imagine that you have a guitar part that needs to fade before every chorus. You could automate this with mixer automation, but the automation would have to include the verse fades and this may not be convenient. Also the verse guitar needs to be identical throughout the song. Create a clip containing the guitar part and use an envelope to draw the fade and other changes. Then duplicate the clip and move the duplicated parts to other verses. The guitar part is now identical for each verse and you still have automation to make changes in the mix.

Editing volume envelopes

1　With View>Enable Clip Envelope Editing enabled choose Show Clip Volume Envelopes from the toolbar.
2　Zoom in vertically until a light green line is visible at the top of any clip.
3　Left click on any clip to select, Edit points appear at the right and left of the light green line.
4　Move the mouse cursor over the green line, the cursor will change to a hand to indicate dragging is possible.
5　Create a diagonal line left to right across the wave by dragging the edit point at the extreme right of the clip down towards the bottom of the block. Playback will now fade out. Create a fade in effect by reversing the line.
6　Click on the line to add more edit points.
7　Remove unwanted edit points by dragging them down past the bottom of the clip.

It's not difficult to create unwanted edit points, or to want to clear points and start again. To clear edit points place the cursor on the envelope and right click, choose Clip Envelopes, Volume (or Pan) and Clear Selected Points.

An alternative to the sawtooth style of envelopes is to use the Spline points option. Splines are gentle curves rather than ramps and can be very subtle. One very good use for splines is to create a pulsing backing track by creating a gentle 2 or 3db bell curve leading to the end of the bar. This creates an almost invisible pumping action which can really help the track along.

Rescaling envelopes

Boosts the volume of a clip and rescales the envelope by the same amount. This can be useful if you have a clip with many edit points and need to boost the overall volume without having to change the position of each point.

Hidden envelope tools

Edit points are added simply by left clicking on the envelope line. New edit points can be moved anywhere along the X or Y axis. There are also three hidden tools.

Shift + Left Click	New Edit Point with vertical motion only
Ctrl + Left Click	Relative Rescale tool. All other edit points are rescaled proportionally to the new edit point. Try this when clicking one end of a flat volume envelope.
Alt + Left Click	Global Change tool. The envelope retains its shape but can be moved vertically up or down the clip.

As the yellow cursor moves over the waveform the clip playback will change according to the changes in the envelope points. When you are satisfied with your envelopes you can remove the edit points to avoid making mistakes while clip dragging etc. Toggle 'Show Clip Volume Envelopes' on the toolbar.

Crossfading clips using envelopes

A useful technique when combining several clips into a performance is to crossfade the volume envelopes of each clip. Crossfading produces the impression that clips are running into each other and produces the feel of a real performance,

1 Arrange clips on alternate tracks
2 Draw volume envelopes on each clip to bring the volume of the next clip up just as the previous clip fades under it.

Alternatively use the Adobe Audition 2.0 crossfade feature to apply crossfades automatically.

1 Arrange the clips on alternate tracks

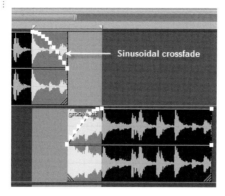

2   Use the time tool to drag select a range over both tracks
3   Left click on the first clip to select it then ctrl + click on the second clip
    to select it also.
4   Right click over the range and select Crossfade, Linear from the menu

Additional options for crossfading tracks include:

Sinusoidal	A curved envelope
Logarithmic	Gradual envelope with a steeper curve towards the end

Envelopes in relation to real time (mixer) Automation

Envelopes pre-date Adobe Audition 2.0, they were created in answer to public demand for some form of automation in Cool Edit Pro. As such they offer a basic form of automation over volume and pan parameters and offer some advantages over mixer automation such as being a lower overhead for the processor etc. Being an old school Cool Edit user I tend to use envelopes over mixer automation because I find that it's usually quicker to draw what I have in mind on the clip rather than start the session rolling and moving the mouse etc. Additionally, the reassuring envelopes on each clip give me a visual clue about what may be happening in the session, something that's not always available - especially if you have automation lanes hidden.

   Real time automation is creating envelope curves using the mixer panel. For instance pan automation can quickly be created over an envelope if you set the target track automation status to 'Write' then adjust the pan control while the track is playing. The difference is that envelopes created in this way are applied to the track as a whole, regardless of the clips or groups of clips on the track. This makes balancing groups of waves very simple. On the other hand a new handle is created for each movement of the control. Creating envelopes in this way produces hundreds of handles which must be processed as the track is playing, causing additional processor load.

   Real time envelopes are displayed in automation lanes under each track. Clip envelopes are displayed on each clip in the track.

Markers and ranges

Markers are points in the track or waveform. They appear as small blue triangles above the waveform and each marker has a blue marker line extending to the ruler. Markers are used in many ways depending on the view and the marker type. Press F8 at any point in the track to create a marker. Markers can be created when the track is playing or not. Right click on any marker to see marker options. Click and drag markers left or right along the track.

Markers placed in the edit view are saved along with the waveform (assuming the option to save non audio information is set. In the multitrack view, markers are saved with the session. Both edit and multitrack markers are shown in the session. This makes it possible for instance to identify a phrase or event in a waveform in the edit view, mark that place and see the marker in the multitrack view. If a marker is placed somewhere along the track in the multitrack view, the edit view marker can be lined up exactly under it. This enables phrases to be matched to video for instance.

Markers in the multitrack and edit view are added to the marker list (Alt +F8). The edit view and multitrack marker list are separate lists. Change marker name and type within the marker list and use the autoplay feature to play from markers from the list.

Ranges

Adding a marker (F8) when a range is selected creates two markers called a range. Ranges are used to identify sections of a song and have numerous uses;

- Create temporary sections for identifying sections of a track that require further attention then delete the range when done. This is as close as Adobe Audition comes at the moment to having a section recall feature.
- Make a range for each song in a compilation session and turn ranges into CD tracks. The ranges are then used in the CD panel when compiling the finished CD.
- Create ranges for each scene in a film production.

Marker types

Markers are assigned types depending on the function of the marker. Change marker type from within the Marker Window (Alt + 8)

Cue. The marker is a flag which is used to identify sections in the session. Cues are added to the marker list and can be edited and named from there. The label appears at the top of the session below the horizontal range bar.

Track. Track markers are used to mark the start of CD tracks. These are read by the CD view when the track is prepared for printing to CD.

Index. Index markers are used by CD players with the ability to read them. They identify the start of sections within a single track. Indexes are most useful when compiling 'live' recordings where the start of each track may not be apparent or songs run into each other.

Beat. Beat markers are used in the edit view for the creation of loops. Adobe Audition uses beat markers when calculating tempo from sections of a waveform. Adobe Audition can also introduce beat markers automatically in the AutoMark feature used in the edit view.

Tip

Using the autoplay feature turns the marker list into a cart or cue list for radio spot effects or theatre.

BWF-J. Inserts BWF (Broadcast Wave Format) timestamp. Broadcast Wave Format is a standard for audio wave file exchange amongst broadcasters. Adobe Audition 2.0 allows timestamp and other metadata to be saved along with the wave file but curiously doesn't have a BWF preset in the file save options. BWF files are 16/48 (16 bit 48k). In order to save files in this format, and with the BWF metadata it's necessary to downsample manually and save including the option to Save Non Audio Information. The non-audio information is stored with the file in the File Info options (Ctrl+P) in the edit view. Adobe Audition 2.0 has full support for BWF and BWF-J (Japanese) metadata.

Creating and using markers in the multitrack view

At any point in the session press the F8 key to create a new marker. Markers are always visible as blue markers above the session. When first created, markers are named sequentially but they can be called anything you like using the cue list.

Marker lines are visible below each marker for use when placing blocks etc. If snapping to markers is enabled (Edit, Snapping) clips will magnetically snap to the nearest marker.

Marker options

Left click and drag any marker elsewhere on the session. Right click on the marker to show other options such as go to the marker list and delete marker.

Ranges can also be used to create markers.

Compiling a CD from a session containing multiple clips

1   Use the time selection tool to create a new range over the area containing the first song in the session.

2   Carefully right click on either of the two yellow split markers at the beginning and end of the range.

3   Choose 'Insert CD Track Marker' from the menu

4   Alternatively press Ctrl+Shift+F8 to create marker

Press Alt + 8 to see the Marker list. Within the list markers can be renamed or changed.

5   Export the entire session using the

mixdown feature (File, Export, Audio Mixdown). When exporting the file ensure that the option to include markers and metadata is enabled.

6 Choose the CD view from the view buttons on the toolbar

7 Drag the new exported wav file from the file panel into the main panel and choose CD options.

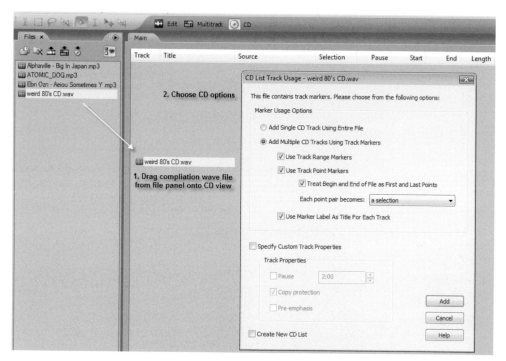

CD tracks are created from ranges within the wave file. Arrange the clips in the session against each other then create ranges for each track so that there is no space between the ranges. Then, when creating the CD you can save time by choosing to have a two second gap inserted automatically between each track instead of having to create numerous two second gaps inside the session.

Exporting cues and markers

Adobe Audition 2.0 markers are saved with the waveform. Also, markers are only saved with files saved in the uncompressed 'wav' format. Markers cannot be saved with mp3 format files.

Other Adobe products such as Premiere pro are not able to read Adobe Audition markers. This is partially a workflow issue. Music and speech are usually dubbed over video, rather than the other way around. When used in this way, Adobe Audition is the perfect tool for creating film and video soundtracks. However, there may be occasions when video events must match music events in the post production suite. Fortunately, Stefan Bion's freeware Cue List Tool is able to extract cue lists from wav files and save them to be imported into other Wavs or even other applications and as such is an essential tool for anyone using Adobe Audition in the music video industry. Download the Cue List Tool from http://www.stefanbion.de.

Using markers as track locators

During a session it's useful to be able to create locators and location ranges which identify portions of a song (Chorus, Verse) a soundtrack (Scene1, Scene 2) or an event in a recording (Birdsong 1, Birdsong 2). Placing locators within a track is usually done with a limited number of preset locate hotkeys Within Adobe Audition markers are used as locators. Markers have the following benefits over simple locators;

- An unlimited number of markers may be produced in the edit view or multitrack
- Markers may be renamed at any time
- Marker type may be changed at any time
- CD selections , files etc. may be produced from markers

As the multitrack or edit view waveform is playing simply tap the F8 key to insert a marker. Drag select over the session or waveform to create a range. Jump to markers from the Marker Window (Alt +8). Double click on any marker or range within the marker window to automatically select that range. Autoplay any marker using the autoplay function in the marker window. Arranging and managing session tracks.

This is now a busy session with multiple clips, loops and recordings in the main panel. A mix could be attempted from this mix as it is. However, the mix engineer or producer would find some difficulties with the number of tracks in the session. Balancing session tracks is quicker if the tracks are arranged in groups (Drums, vocals, strings). Session clips need to be balanced and the session needs to be arranged to make sense when lined up in the mixer panel.

The session can be made simpler in two ways.

- New track length waveforms can be compiled from tracks with multiple clips. This technique is called bouncing down.
- Groups of tracks can be sorted into 'stems'

A stem is a collection of tracks with something in common. For instance the drums may lie across eight or more tracks. These could be arranged and sent to one stereo buss. Horns or percussion or backing vocals can also create stem tracks. The material inside the stem can still be balanced and mixed down. But the engineer only has to worry about one pair of stereo levels for a group of many tracks. It's common now for record companies to request the stems as separate stereo tracks, falong with the finished album or track mix. This enables the record company to ask other producers and engineers to create other mixes for other purposes from the stem tracks.

Bouncing tracks

Tracks containing large numbers of separate clips can be 'bounced' into a complete track length waveform. This is often preferable to having a large number of potentially fragile clips in a single track. Bounced tracks inherit all the attributes of the clips that are used to create them. So system resources can be conserved by creating a bounced track containing a number of clips complete with effects, volume and pan envelopes etc.

Bouncing clips from a single track

- Right click over any free space in the track. Choose 'Select all clips in track' from the right click menu.
- Right click again. Choose bounce to new track.

The options in this menu will change depending on the selected clips. Always, you'll see options for stereo and mono. Bouncing a stereo file to mono will lose more in quality and depth than you'll gain in system resources.

Choosing 'All Audio Clips in session' ignores your clip selection and grabs all the clips in the entire session into a single stereo (or mono) waveform. If you want to you can select a range using the time tool or left click and drag. Then bouncing to a new track will produce another option 'all clips in selected range' This option can be useful, maybe if you have a great four or eight beat drum performance that you'd like to turn into a loop. In this case one way to achieve it would be to solo the drum tracks and select the particular break that you need using the range tool. Then bounce down just the selected range and use the new waveform for your loops.

The new file containing the 'bounced' tracks is inserted into the multitrack near to the selected source clips.

Exporting audio

Stem tracks can be created using the export function. Exporting tracks outside of Adobe Audition enables the tracks to be saved in alternative formats and to alternative locations. Right click over any empty space in the track and choose 'Export to File' from the right click menu. This is the same feature as found in the File Menu (File, Export, Audio Mixdown) although exporting from track options presets some of the options in the file export dialog. For instance only the contents of that track will be exported (although this can

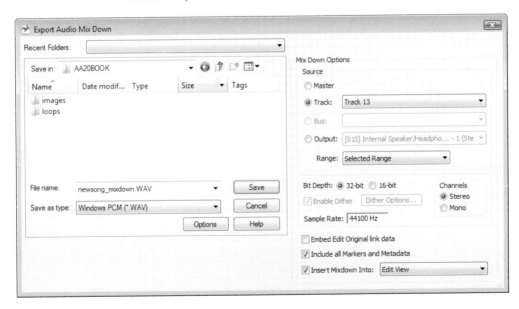

easily be changed from within the dialog). If a range has been created, the mix down dialog will also select that as the default option. The difference between exporting audio in this way, and bouncing tracks is that the bounced track always inherits the session sample rate and bit depth. The audio export option on the other hand allows for the new wave to be downsampled if necessary and also for a different folder to be chosen as the target.

Insert time

Most of the options on the right click menu in the track window are duplicated from other menus in the program. For instance if you want to solo or mute a track, it's much more convenient to do this in the track controls with one click, rather than having to right click – and then left click within the track. But one useful feature has been hidden away at the bottom of this menu.

Insert time splits all tracks and clips at the cursor point and introduces a measure of free space, either in bars or in decimal time. This is useful in sessions which need to be split into tracks, for creating a CD etc. or where the song has no count in. Type the number of bars or beats into the Insert/Delete time dialog. For instance; if you wish to insert 8 bars type the number 8. Alternatively the delete time function can be used to remove sections of the session. The option to delete time only appears when a range has been selected.

MIDI tracks

Adobe Audition works with the operating system to enable MIDI file playback (not creating or editing) of MIDI files from within the multitrack view. Adobe Audition is also able to react to triggers produced by a sequencer or any other MIDI equipment and transmitted to the computer over MIDI. Additionally, Adobe Audition is able to act as a master or a slave device in a SMPTE/MTC sync situation.

MIDI data enters the PC through a MIDI interface. This may be an external device featuring numerous MIDI input and output connections such as a USB Midisport or similar. Alternatively the PC may have a MIDI socket as a feature of the internal soundcard.

MIDI/ SMPTE sync is only possible in the multitrack view.

Tip

If you can't seem to get MIDI to work at all check the connections where your MIDI cables meet your computer and where the MIDI cable meets your equipment. MIDI sockets are one-way either in or out of the device. For MIDI information to get into the computer it's necessary for the MIDI out of your equipment to meet the MIDI input of your computer and vice-versa. Two MIDI cables are usual, one for MIDI in and one for MIDI out. Connect the MIDI output of your controller keyboard or device to the MIDI in of the computer sound card. Connect the MIDI out of the computer sound card to the MIDI in of any tone module.

Because MIDI cables do not carry audio data it is impossible to record the sound of any MIDI keyboard even when the MIDI cables are connected. MIDI only enables the software inside the keyboard to talk to software inside another keyboard or computer etc. Audio cables must be connected to hear the sound of the equipment.

MIDI file formats

Adobe Audition provides MIDI functionality limited to playback of MIDI files (Type 0 and 1). Type O MIDI files contains data in just one track. Type 1 MIDI files contain data in any number of tracks. Both types of MIDI file transmit data on 16 channels. Adobe Audition is able to decode and pass data from the MIDI file to any internal or external MIDI device.

Opening and controlling playback properties of a MIDI file

Within the multitrack view start a new session and choose Insert>MIDI From File from the menu bar. Browse and select any MIDI file. The MIDI file is automatically inserted in the first free track. Alternatively use the Navigator (Alt + 9) and drag a currently loaded MIDI file from the Navigator to anywhere within the session. MIDI blocks are similar to waveblocks in that they may be split and duplicated etc. but MIDI blocks do not have loop properties.

Playback properties for the MIDI file may be adjusted using the right click menu. The entire MIDI block may be transposed using 'Transpose' or MIDI Tempo may be changed using 'Set Tempo' In this way the overall playback speed of the MIDI file may be changed to suit the tempo of the track. Tempo information contained in the MIDI file may be seen by choosing View>Show Tempo Envelopes from the title bar or by choosing the appropriate button from the Menu Bar.

MIDI mapping

Mapping instruments to MIDI channels enables the user to control which device or port a particular instrument will be sent to. MIDI devices (internal and external) have 16 channels each. Some MIDI controllers or interfaces have more than one MIDI output port. Additionally your system soundcard probably has a GM (General MIDI) synthesiser built in. Use the MIDI mapping feature to control which instruments are sent to which port. For instance you may have a dedicated MIDI drum module on Port A and a General MIDI synth (with less dramatic drum sounds) on Port B. In this case the drum parts from the MIDI file (usually on Channel 10) would be mapped to Port A while all the other instruments are mapped to Port B. See MIDI Mapping options by pressing the MAP button within the track controls bar in the multitrack view (the map button is only present for MIDI tracks). Choose an instrument from the top of the dialog and choose a Device and channel to map to from the lower two boxes. Channels without alternative mapping are simply transmitted on their default channel. Shift-click to select more than one instrument. If you wish to re-map an entire MIDI file to another port it is necessary to select the whole 16 channels.

Active tracks

If necessary just one channel may be selected for playback using the active tracks feature (right click menu over any MIDI track in the multitrack view). The active track data is highlighted within the MIDI track.

Controller 7 value

MIDI Controller 7 is the Volume controller for each MIDI channel.

Volume envelopes over a MIDI block

Adobe Audition enables drawing of volume envelopes over a MIDI block in the same way as envelopes may be drawn over a waveblock. This is a convenient way of creating fades, etc.

SMPTE / MTC synchronisation

Syncing to external video or audio equipment is enabled by the use of SMPTE (Society of Motion Picture and Television Engineers) Time Code over MTC (MIDI Time Code). In this way SMPTE time code is encoded into the MIDI traffic. SMPTE over MTC is a convenient method of sending and receiving time code without having to purchase expensive SMPTE equipment. When syncing to external devices Adobe Audition may function as a master controller or slave. Time code is transmitted and received via MIDI. The host computer must be fitted with a MIDI controller and MIDI sockets.

SMPTE options

SMPTE functionality is enabled within the multitrack view from the options menu. Alternatively use keyboard shortcuts to turn SMPTE sync on or off.

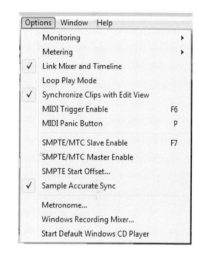

To enable Adobe Audition as a SMPTE slave:

- Connect the SMPTE or MIDI output of the master device to the MIDI in socket of the PC.
- Ensure that the frame rate of the master device matches the frame rate used by the Adobe Audition session. Right click over the Display Time window to see frame options.
- Enable the PC as SMPTE Slave by choosing SMPTE Slave Enable from the Options menu in the multitrack view or by pressing F7 on the keyboard.
- Set the master device running.
- Adobe Audition will playback automatically from 0:00:00:00 or will wait for a valid offset before playback. Set playback offset in Advanced Session Properties.

MIDI commands are echoed in the bottom left border in the status window.

SMPTE offset

It is very unusual for both the session and the movie to start at 00:00:00:00 exactly. More likely is that the movie soundtrack needs to wait for titles or headers. At the video playback device note the SMPTE time at the point just before the soundtrack should begin. Then enter that value in the SMPTE offset value in Advanced Session Properties.

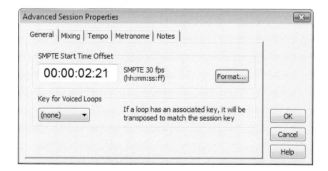

- Select SMPTE offset from the Options Menu.
- Choose the SMPTE frame rate from the format.
- Read the time in hours, minutes, seconds and frames from the external video playback
- Copy this into the offset

Playback will now be delayed until this timeframe is received at the MIDI input.

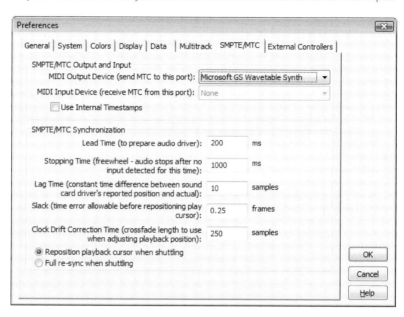

Lead time	Adobe Audition will use this time to prepare audio sync. Transport is always delayed by thisperiod in milliseconds after a start message is received from the master device.
Stopping time	Transport will always continue for this period after the sync signal is no longer detected.
Lag time	Adobe Audition internal time will always be this number of samples later than the incoming time frame.
Slack Time	Adobe Audition will wait for this long before repositioning the start position (playback) cursor if a difference in sync is detected.
Clock Drift Correction time	This amount of crossfading will be used when the playback cursor is repositioned.
Reposition Cursor/Full Resync	Is the action that Adobe Audition will take when the sync drifts further than the allowance in the slack time option. Simple repositioning will place the cursor where Adobe Audition estimates it should now be. Full Resync forces Adobe Audition to sync again with the incoming time signal.

Use SMPTE settings in Settings>Device Properties when troubleshooting sync problems between master and slave devices. The two most useful values in this dialog are Stopping Time and Slack time. If synching the PC with an older machine the Slack Time value allows for drift in the SMPTE code before Adobe Audition makes a guess and repositions the playback cursor to where it thinks it should be. Stopping Time allows Adobe Audition to keep going for a short period of time in case of dropouts or some other failure when reading time code.

Configuring Adobe Audition 2.0 as a MIDI master

Adobe Audition 2.0 can control any MIDI device that can accept SMPTE or MTC:

1 Connect the MIDI out port of the host Adobe Audition computer to the MIDI in port of the receiving equipment.
2 Enable MIDI master sync from the Options menu.
3 Press play on the transport to start sending MTC information.

MIDI triggering

Any MIDI controller device (keyboard, guitar, drums, etc.) can be used to control features and functions including controlling playback, recording, effects, etc.

* Choose Keyboard Shortcuts / MIDI triggers from the Edit menu and select the required input device and data channel.
* Use the mouse to click on any command name in the list.
* Send the MIDI trigger data to the MIDI port using your keyboard, MPC, etc.
* Enable MIDI triggering in the multitrack (F6)

The MIDI note and channel appears in the MIDI trigger column alongside any enabled command. Each command may be enabled for edit view, multitrack view or the CD view. If the MIDI triggering appears not to work it may be that these options are incorrect. MIDI triggering needs to be enabled in for Adobe Audition to accept commands from the MIDI device. MIDI reception can be confirmed by looking at the lower left corner of the Adobe Audition status bar. A MIDI Triggering message can be seen followed by real time MIDI information whenever a key is pressed. If no real time information can be seen then Adobe Audition 2.0 is not receiving information from the external device or sound card. In this case the connections and settings must be checked.

Using SMPTE sync as an audio solution

Utilising SMPTE sync can help solve a recently recurring problem, e.g: You have an old eight track multitrack recorder and some valuable recordings which you'd like to clean up and remix in the digital domain. The problem is that while it is possible to simply make four stereo passes into Adobe Audition, all four will be out of sync because varying motor speed and tape stretch mean that each pass will drift out of time. The solution is to lose one of the eight tracks, perhaps a backing vocal or percussion part that can easily be replaced. Using an external SMPTE generator stripe the newly created free track with SMPTE along the length of the tape. Enable SMPTE slave and connect the MIDI out of the external sync box to MIDI in of the PC. The SMPTE code will have to be translated by the sync box into SMPTE or MTC over MIDI. With the SMPTE timing locked to the tape Adobe Audition will follow the timing drift accurately and the transfer can be achieved.

Tip

Choosing a frame rate of 29.97FPS (SMPTE Drop Frame) causes SMPTE to drop three frames each minute. This will cause errors in playback *no matter* how lag or slack times are set. This setting caused me much frustration until I figured out what I was doing wrong and swapped to a standard 25FPS.

Tip

MIDI triggering must be enabled for each command in turn as there are different properties for each item.

Creating markers for video 'spot effects'

Creating spot effects or synchronising speech to film requires the insertion of cues either as the video is playing or when playback has stopped (press F8 to manually insert a cue at any time). Use the Zoom to Selection button on the transport bar to close right in on any section of playback. Pressing the Fast Forward or Rewind button on the transport bar enables 'scrubbing' over any small section. Choose SMPTE (24fps) by right clicking over the display time window and enable snapping to Cues only (Edit>Snapping). Waveblocks can then be aligned with sample accuracy to any point in the video.

The mixer panel

With recorded waveforms, loops and other items in the multitrack session, it's time to consider how the various elements could combine to create the audio production. Adobe Audition allows you to create simple balance mixes using the track controls. Additionally you can use clip properties and envelopes to adjust the output and pan of each waveblock or clip. The mixer expands on these controls and enables the production of finished audio recorded and mixed entirely within the PC ('in the box').

The mixer panel is laid in the usual way with the source at the top of the panel. EQ and effects underneath the input. Pan and fader below the EQ. The mixer panel is a convenient way to see properties for every track and also as a tool to balance, add effects and EQ and even automate changes to any part of the mix as it plays.

Adobe Audition gain stages

Jump right in and use the mixer panel. It's laid out in the traditional way and is easy and intuitive to use. Mixing and balancing in the PC ('in the box') is always intended to look and feel just like mixing using analogue controls. However the technology underneath is completely different. A little reading right now will help you get the best from the tools provided in this powerful application.

Amplitude is volume. Waveblocks containing samples with high amplitudes are 'louder' than waveforms containing low amplitude samples. The amplitude of the sample is simply an instruction to the digital analogue converters contained in the soundcard. The soundcard reproduces the waveform with more or less power depending on the instructions received. Amplitude is measured in dBfs (DeciBels Full Scale) with 0 db being the maximum amplitude for the waveform. Instructions to store data above that point are reproduced as distortion. Digital distortion is called clipping.

The level meters in Adobe Audition 2.0 are an important reference when recording or reproducing waveforms. If clipping occurs the peak indicators will glow red. Maintain levels that stay in the green with peaks in the orange section. Click on the red clip indicators to clear if necessary.

Individual waveblock amplitude should be attenuated or boosted using clip properties (Right Click over the waveblock, choose Properties.)

Envelopes can be used to attenuate levels from groups of waves but envelopes cannot boost the level of the waveform above the limit set in clip properties.

Track controls and the mixer are the same stage. Changing volume and pan in the track controls also causes the controls in the mixer to change. Track controls and the mixer are used to balance the levels coming from the entire track, not individual waveforms.

Signal to noise

Recordings always contain a certain amount of background noise. Noise can be part of the recording environment, or it may be generated by the equipment used to make the recording (microphones, pre-amps and recorders etc.). The music or speech is always recorded in relation to this noise. For instance if you record a speech in a noisy hall, the speakers voice may be indistinct. Raising the amplitude of the waveform will not make the speakers voice any clearer as the background noise will also be amplified in relation.

Faders on the mixer panel can boost the amplitude of the waveform but at the expense of headroom and detail. Use clip properties to ensure that each waveblock produces a peak level of -6db maximum with an average of -30db minimum. Use Alt+7 to view the master level window.

Manage levels in your tracks

- Use clip properties to balance 'loud' (high amplitude) waves with 'quiet' (low amplitude) waves. Waves requiring more than 10db of cut or boost in order to balance with adjoining waveforms should be modified in the edit view. When the track is playing there should be just minor variations in the levels coming from adjoining waveblocks.
- Use envelopes to manage crossfades between waveblocks or detailed changes in level along the length of the track. It's not possible to create one envelope over a group of tracks or to create a envelope along the length of a track.
- Use the mixer to govern the level of the track as it balances with the mix.
- Use mixer automation for creative balancing and mixing, such as crossfading between tracks.

Using the mixer

The mixer panel is hidden behind the Main panel in the default multitrack view. Click on the mixer tab next to the main tab to reveal the mixer.

Each track in the Main panel has a corresponding track in the Mixer Panel. MIDI tracks don't have EQ and effects but do have a volume control. Video tracks do not appear in the mixer.

Track name

Overtype the track contents here. Track Names are used to name recorded waveforms so it's a good idea to name tracks before recording as the saved waveblocks will be easy to identify.

Input device

In record mode only. The input device is the default device chosen in Audio Hardware Setup. Choose an alternative input device or port from the drop down menu. Pressing and holding Shift + Ctrl changes the input device for every track.

Phase

Reverses the phase of the incoming signal. Useful when recording Mid-Side or for resolving problems with multi-microphone setups.

Level control

Although a level control is provided, this has no effect on levels received from the soundcard. Boosting the level when recording will create clipping at the output device but recording levels will remain constant, The Level Control affects playback only.

FX on /off

Turns the effects rack globally on or off.

FX pre or post fader

Effects that are placed pre-fader are not affected by track volume. For instance, inserting a long reverb into a track and then having that effect post-fader produces a long tail for the reverb when the fader is lowered. If the effect is placed pre-fader the effect will fade out along with the dry part of the signal as the fader is lowered.

For instance; if you have a send to Bus A and that Bus has a reverb effect placed in line, you can listen to the sound of just the wet reverb by setting the Send pre-fader and the Reverb Bus to Post-Fader. Solo the reverb buss and mute the send in the track controls. Only the wet reverb sound is heard as the send is now pre-fader; when the mute is applied the send is still active.

Freeze tracks

The speed of the host computers processor and other parts of the system limits the amount of effects that can be used in a session. If the number of effect used exceeds the computers ability to process the data in good time, the session will appear to stall or even stop. The number of effects that can be used can be increased by the use of the Freeze Tracks feature. This creates a temporary file containing the track and the effects. Adobe Audition 2.0 then uses this file rather than processing the effects in real time. Use the Freeze Track option whenever you have a track which does not have to change, a slapback delay and compressor rack on a bass for instance. The effects can change but the track has to be unfrozen. To unfreeze a track, press the Freeze button again. Only effects are frozen, EQ, automation and fader can still be altered in real time.

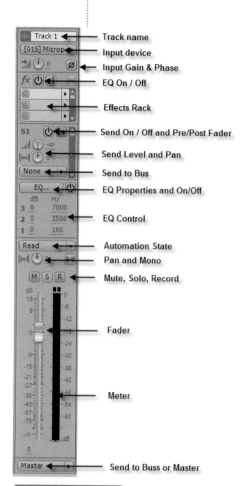

- Track name
- Input device
- Input Gain & Phase
- EQ On / Off
- Effects Rack
- Send On / Off and Pre/Post Fader
- Send Level and Pan
- Send to Bus
- EQ Properties and On/Off
- EQ Control
- Automation State
- Pan and Mono
- Mute, Solo, Record
- Fader
- Meter
- Send to Buss or Master

Listen to the sound of just the wet reverb by setting the Send pre-fader and the Reverb Bus to Post-Fader.

Effects rack

Double click on any blank entry in the effects rack to produce the effects rack. If the effects rack is empty you will see the default effects rack for that track. Double click on any effect in the effects rack to see that effect only. It's not possible to see multiple effects (Reason style) in the effects rack. Click on the twistie against each entry to see a list of VST, Direct X and Process effects available. Each effect is added to the list underneath the previous effect. The effects rack in the mixer is the same effects rack as in the track controls.

Double click on any blank entry in the effects rack to produce the effects rack.

Effects and the default session

Inconveniently, there is no default effects rack in Adobe Audition 2.0. Each effects rack must be set up for each track which can be a little time consuming, especially if you use the same effects for certain tracks in every session. The solution to this is to set up the effects and tracks as you like and save the session as the default. Adobe Audition creates each new session using the settings in the default session. Therefore it's a convenient way to create a standard workspace for each new session. Multiple effects have a significant processor load. Saving multiple effects into the default session can make the session very slow to load.

Create a new default session as follows:

- Start a new (empty) session.
- Populate the new session with effects, busses and track names.
- From the menu bat choose File, Default Session, Set Current Session as Default

The new session sample rate dialogue provides the option not to load the default session if necessary. Remove the check mark from the box at the bottom of the dialogue. If necessary, empty the default session using the option File, Default Session, Clear default session.

Effects types in Adobe Audition 2.0

Adobe Audition hosts four different types of effects.

Adobe Audition 'native' effects

Native effects are real time effects built into Adobe Audition. They aren't VST or Direct X. Native effects can be used in real time and so are enabled for the effects rack.

Process effects

Process effects are native Adobe Audition effects, built into the program. Most of these effects were developed for Adobe Audition 1 and Cool Edit Pro. Process effects do not render in real time, they must be applied over an effect in the edit view. The process effects are very high quality and include the scientific effects such as the pitch corrector and scientific filters.

VST effects

Adobe Audition is a VST host and so can host any of the millions of VST effects available for purchase or for free. Adobe Audition can't handle poorly written VST effects and will crash out if particularly badly written effects are loaded.

Direct X

Direct X is a Microsoft layer. Adobe Audition support the use of Direct X effects which must be installed outside of the program. Refresh the effects list after each new Direct X effect is installed.

Managing the effects rack

The effects rack can host 16 effects. Effects are processed in order, in other words the effect that is last in the chain will process all of the other effects present in the chain. Effects work with each other in the same way that a guitarist would use effects pedals in a chain. For this reason, the effects rack is better when used for sound shaping insert effects such as compression and filters rather than delay effects. Create a reverb buss and use the send controls in each track to send to that buss, rather than using multiple instances in effects racks. Within the effects rack the order of the effects can be changed by grabbing the effect name and dragging the effect up or down in the list. The order of the effects is important to how the rack will sound. Input levels into the rack and output to mixer can also be adjusted from this panel. The mix control underneath the output fader controls how much of the dry signal is returned to the mix. As this is the effects rack it's normal to leave this at 100%. In this state the effects rack is acting as an insert effect.

Effects parameters can be saved and recalled individually or globally as a rack preset. Rack Presets contain all the effects parameters for all of the effects in the rack and are stored in the 2.0 folder containing the Adobe Audition preferences. Effects rack presets can be loaded into any other session. Settings for individual effects can be saved. These are saved alongside the other effects presets with the VST instrument.

Track send

Sending routes a portion of the track to a buss track. Use sends when apply-ing processor intensive complex effects to a session. Each track can have up to sixteen sends. Sends only route to Bus tracks, never to other tracks. However, Bus tracks can also route to Bus tracks. In this way you can create a complex bus system with one overall effects return.

Each Send has a Level and Pan control. The Level and Pan controls change the values for that send only to the Bus track.

Mousing over the rotary controls

The rotary controls in Adobe Audition 2.0 respond to mouse acceleration. Slow movements produce tiny incremental adjustments to the control while fast movements produce large travel in the control.

Click on the control and move the mouse pointer vertically to change the value. Or click on the numeric value and overtype another value directly into the control. Type 0 (zero) to return controls to dead centre.

Pressing and holding the Alt key while clicking on any rotary control returns that control to dead centre.

Track EQ

Each track has a simple three band EQ. This is a basic EQ for non scientific EQ of simple tracks. For advanced sound shaping or problem solving load notch filtering and parametric EQ effects into the effects rack.

Each frequency band has a horizontal frequency slider and a vertical fader by which cut or boost can be applied to the selected frequency. Alternatively the three handles on the EQ graph may be dragged to select frequency and boost or cut. The graph shows low frequencies to the left and high frequen-cies to the right.

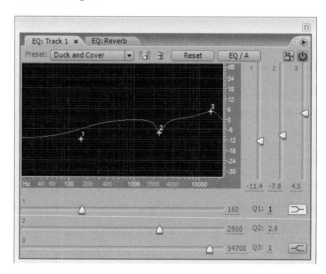

Track EQ is a three band EQ with adjustable Q for the mid frequencies. Each band has adjustable Q with the high and low frequencies also having high and low shelving respectively. If shelving is enabled the Q is set at 1 for that band. Q is the shape of the EQ curve. Very high Q produces a sharp spike of cut or boosted frequencies. Low Q produces a bell curve. A Q of 1 produces a natural sounding curve. Apply shelving to EQ if you need to boost or reduce the level of all frequencies above or below a particular point. For instance; remove muddiness from a bass guitar or drum track by applying a low EQ shelf at around 40Hz. Frequencies below 40 Hz can be attenuated (reduced) dramatically using 30 or 40db's of cut without affecting the valuable mid sections of the track at all.

Most EQ problem solving happens in the mid frequencies (500Hz - 2500kHz) and this is where a variable Q can be useful . For instance, to notch out a particular frequency produced by a resonant room first produce a spike of around 2 or 3 Q in the mid band with a boost of 15db. Use the fader to sweep up and down the frequency band until the troublesome frequency is identified then reverse the EQ and cut by 5 to 7db. Narrow Q settings can produce unnatural effects, broaden the Q to include the troublesome band of frequencies without unnaturally affecting the sound of the track.

EQ can be switched on or off using the power button. Compare alternative EQ settings or 'curves' for the same track using the EQ/A button. The EQ section has two separate EQ curves; EQ A and EQ /B. Clicking over the EQ /A button switches to EQ /B. This feature enables different curves to be created and then applied independently for comparison. Create an alternative EQ curve in EQ /B and switch between them to examine the effect of different curves on the same piece of music. Curves can be reset at any time by pressing the reset button. Favourite EQ settings can be saved and recalled at any time using the standard floppy disk icon to save and the dustbin icon to remove presets.

The track EQ frame contains the EQ settings for all tracks in the session. Enabling EQ in other tracks creates additional tabs in the EQ Frame. Right click over any tab and select Undock Panel to create additional EQ panels.

Tip

Effects and EQ dialogs have a small padlock button. Enabling this padlock protects EQ or effect settings against being changed accidentally when automation is written.

Pan and mono controls
Adobe Audition 2.0 by default will attenuate track level by -3db when the pan control is in the central position. This is to overcome the natural summing of levels in the stereo field. This behaviour can be changed in system preferences; Edit – Preferences (F4). If you want to preserve levels when pan control is central choose the option for Left/Right Cut Logarithmic.

Mono
Stereo waveforms in a track can be summed to mono using the mono button. Useful for placing synth lines recorded in stereo into a complex stereo field.

Mute, solo, record
- Mute; mutes (turns off) that track only.
- Solo; mutes all other tracks. Only the solo track and track output is heard.
- Record; arms that track for record.

Pressing and holding Shift + Ctrl while clicking over any track mute, solo or record buttons sets the same option for every track.

Fader

Boosts or attenuates the output of that track. Moving the fader above the 0 marker produces an additional 15db of gain.

Press and hold the Alt key while clicking on the fader button to return the fader to 0. Press and hold the alt key while clicking anywhere on the fader calibration will cause the fader to smoothly move to that new location. This can be recorded with track automation.

Track meters

Moving representations of level produced by that track. If Adobe Audition 2.0 is in Audition Mix mode (Session Properties Panel) the faders will respond to input levels coming into Adobe Audition when the track is armed. Right click over the meters to see global metering options. The defaults are 72db dynamic range and dynamic peaks.

Creating an effects buss

A buss is a common path. In mixer terms it means a channel set aside for an effect. Routing (sending) a portion of a track to a buss means that the amount of reverb returned to the mix can be changed with one fader and also that a heavy plugin can be shared among many tracks.

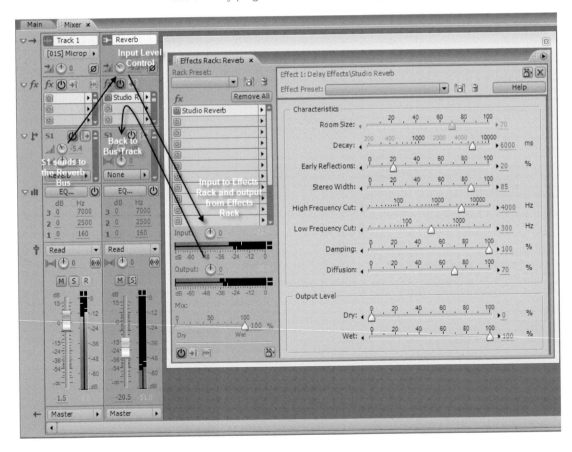

- Click over the output menu for S1 and choose 'Add Bus' from the menu
- The new Bus track appears after the last empty track
- Double click in the Effects Rack of the Bus track and choose an effect
- Use the S1 Level control to send level to the Bus track
- Mix the signal back from the Bus using the Bus track fader

Mix effects from the Effects track 100% wet in the Bus track. Monitor levels coming into the Bus track carefully as excessive gain will cause the wrong type of distortion. Click and drag the small fader to the right of S1 to reveal additional track sends. Each track can send to up to 16 Bus tracks

Creating track reverb

Placing instruments and performers in the same three dimensional space brings the separate tracks into the same domain and creates a believable stage for the song or session. Create a buss track with one high quality reverb in which a medium to large room has been created. Mix the reverb 100% wet, no dry signal should be present in the buss track. Use sends from each track to send a portion of that track to the reverb space. Place performers or instruments inside that space in relation to each other and to the room using varying amounts of send from each track.

Balancing and routing the session mix

The production of commercial music generally begins with the creating of various 'beds' within the completed track. A 'bed' is a group of tracks which on their own will stand up as a musical piece. When these beds are combined the production is formed from these individual pieces.

Music beds

Rhythmic

Buss1: Kick, Snare, Toms, Cymbals
Buss2: Overheads, Ambient mics
Buss3: Loops, percussion, samples, DJ
Buss4: Bass guitar, Rhythm guitar, Organ

Melodic

Buss1: String pads, ambient pads
Buss2: Blown instruments (flutes, reeds)

Harmonic

Buss1: Backing vocals, accapellas
Buss2: Sampled choirs, choir pads
Buss3: Horn stabs, pick guitar, effects

Feature

Buss1: Lead Vocals (possibly comped from two or three tracks)
Buss2: Other vocals (rapping, etc)

With the creation of these four beds, and the individual bus tracks that make up the beds, the production is now a sum of manageable parts. The bed approach makes the production of complex parts much simpler. In addition the record company may request that these beds (or stems) are supplied along with the finished master mix. In this way the record company or publisher can supply the beds to other producers or agencies, for instance if the track is to be used for an advertisement.

Creating the buss tracks and grouping into beds

Rhythm: Arrange the tracks logically to put Kick, Snare and other kit parts together on adjacent tracks. Tracks can easily be moved by clicking on the left of the track name and dragging vertically up or down the list of tracks in the main panel or horizontally in the mixer panel. Bus tracks can also be moved in this way. If not already named, name each track (click on the track name).

A buss track needs to be created for each component of the bed. Buss tracks are easily created by right clicking on the output device section of one track and choosing Add Buss from the menu. The Buss track is created and placed next to the master output track in. Assignments can be seen at the bottom of each track in

the mixer panel. Create and name a new Buss called 'Kit' and select this buss as the output device for each part of the kit (Bass, Snare, Toms, etc.).

Now the kit parts are routed correctly you can begin to balance the kit. Set each fader to 0 (Alt click on the fader top) and add effects and EQ where necessary.

Tip

Create additional buss tracks for reverb and other dimensional effects. Route to these bus tracks from the track sends. Drastic EQ curves can be created on a Buss track. This works great for Ambient and Overhead tracks and saves processor load.

Critically examine each track

Individually listen to each track; kick drum, snare, etc. and apply small amounts of EQ if necessary to shape the sound of the parts. It shouldn't be necessary to add more than 4-5db of cut or boost at this stage. The track EQ's aren't powerful enough for real problem solving and because they are real time effects, they add additional processor loads. If the track requires drastic EQ, consider applying EQ to the waveform in the edit view rather than at the mixer stage. Level meters for every track with EQ and effects should peak no more than -6db.

Work your way along the mixer editing and changing effect and EQ values until the kit parts sound as you'd like them to. Every change should be heard not only with other tracks muted but also carefully with the other tracks. A small 2db boost at 400Hz across kick, snare, toms and a pair of overheads adds up to a massive 10db of low mid boost across the whole kit. Most importantly, any EQ change affects not just the sound of that track but the whole song. Always look at EQ from the top down.

When mixing, your aim should always be to balance EQ, effects and level for the track, then for the buss or group, then for the mix. You can easily tell if your balance is going in the right direction. If each fader is near enough 0db, give or take 4 or 5db when playing back a basic balance (without automation or fades etc.), you have balanced EQ and effects correctly. If, when playing your listening mix, your faders are compensating for too much boost, or too little level, then your EQ and effects need to be revisited.

Now the kit is balanced and routed to the Kit buss tracks, the whole kit can be balanced using just the buss faders. At this point you may also freeze the effects for that track. When a track is frozen, Adobe Audition 2.0 creates a temporary waveform for that track. Effects and EQ values are rendered into the temporary waveform. This reduces processor load by removing the need for effects and EQ values to be calculated for that track. Because the resources used by frozen tracks are returned to the system, more effects can be used in the whole mix. To Freeze a track click the 'freeze' button to the right of the EQ power button.

Repeat this process for each other bed in your arrangement;

1 Create a Buss track for the new bed and route individual tracks to the buss
2 Solo each track in turn
3 Use clip properties to balance clips with other clips.
4 Use envelopes to create crossfades between clips and waveblocks
5 Use Effects and EQ to build the sound of your track
6 Use the mixer section to automate performance changes.
7 Freeze the track
8 Use the Buss controls to balance the bed against other beds in the arrangement.

Balance the tracks and beds

No right or wrong way exists to balance and mix a track or audio production. The relative levels of each track, the amount of EQ and effects and the plac-ing of parts in the stereo field are decisions which need to be made by the producer. However there are a few simple traps which may be avoided by everyone producing audio, whether for film, soundtrack or music production.

Quote

'If you can't take the room out of the mix, you can't take the mix out of the room'

This high brow statement assumes that everyone producing music has access to scientifically designed audio environments which don't in any way colour the sound of the recordings. Of course, this is only true for a small number of the people producing music in the world. A huge number of famous and extremely successful recordings have been made in front rooms, bathrooms and open fields. On the other hand, mixing and balancing tracks in a room or environment with serious audio problems is a waste of time since your productions simply won't translate 'outside of the room'.

Everyone producing audio should go as far as they can to ensure that the listening environment in which production decisions are made is as acoustically 'flat' as possible. At one extreme this might mean structural alterations to the control room. For instance room resonance is the nature of a room in terms of audio frequency. Every room will enhance certain frequencies. If the engineer is unaware of this effect the mix will contain frequency compensation in terms of larger than necessary EQ adjustments. Outside of the control room these EQ decisions will jump out, either as too much bass or a muddy and undefined mix. The worst sort of room to mix or balance in is a simple cube. A cube has walls and ceilings of equal proportions which act together to enhance frequencies. A 'perfect' room has walls and ceilings which don't share the same dimensions.

Structural alterations in terms of replacing walls and ceilings is way beyond the ability of most producers. Mixing with a pair of very high quality headphones is a very good alternative. A pair of headphones with a very flat response enables the engineer to identify problems with the mix before printing and is a much more available solution to the problem of room resonance.

Professional EQ

Audio professionals talk about 'making holes' in EQ values for other instruments to fit into. For instance Hip Hop and R&B producers aim to create EQ shapes and curves on the kick drum track for the bass track to slot into. Use this principle on other tracks and groups of instruments. For instance much of the energy in an orchestral sound is in the mid range. The bottom end can nearly always be shelved off. A complimentary sound such as a low synth pad can slot into this low end without disturbing the sound of the orchestra, but at the same time fooling the ear into believing that the orchestral sound is much richer than it actually is.

When making audio for streaming or podcasts consider that although the frequency response for in-ear type headphones is in the range 20Hz to 20kHz, the actual response is actually much narrower, particularly in the bass end when it can be as high as 50Hz depending on the model of headphones and the nature of the wearers ear canal. Because of this, recordings for podcasts can be limited to a much narrower band of frequencies than audio destined for a good consumer hi-fi system.

Transparency

Every audio track contains a certain amount of noise. The appearance of noise just before the part warns the ear that the part is on the way and so enables us to mentally prepare. While this is a terrific advantage when looking out for attack in a dark forest or jungle, fooling the mind by removing the advance warning is a terrific way to introduce impact into your production.

Use clip edge dragging to drag the edges of clips to a couple of milliseconds before the start of the audio and use clip envelopes to remove unwanted breath sounds or other noises between phrases.

Adobe Audition 2.0 noise reduction algorithms are among the best in the world and can easily be used to remove background noise, hiss or interference. Noise reduction and other audio restoration tool s are process effects and used in the edit view.

Drag the clip edge to the start of the phrase

The master track

All tracks and Busses are routed to one stereo pair called the master track. The master track governs the overall level of the session and the default output device in hardware. The master track does not render the mix as a stereo waveform within Adobe Audition 2.0. If you need Adobe Audition to render a complete stereo waveform within the box, you must choose the Export option (File, Export, Audio Mix-Down) and then import the wave back into Audition, or simply choose the option to place the mixdown file onto a new track in the multitrack view.

From the master track the session is printed as a new waveform or routed outside of the program to an external hardware device for further routing to a recorder etc. Click on the menu below the fader in the master track to see hardware options.

Tip

Adobe Audition 2.0 workflow can be confusing if you're used to working with non-linear analogue or digital mixers. If you want to print a finished mix, it's not necessary to play the track end to end. Exporting the mix as a stereo file does this job for you, just much quicker. This makes sense when thinking about feature length projects such as albums or film soundtracks. The completed project can be printed in a fraction of the time that it would take to listen to it end to end. It's only when using Adobe Audition to print to an external recording device that you will need to run the session end to end.

Layout

The master track (right) is laid out in the same way as the other tracks with the exception of a phase inversion tool at the top of the track and with the session elapsed time displayed underneath the master fader. Mastering effects and EQ can be applied in the master track but sends are not available. Master tracks cannot be frozen.

Automation can be applied to the master track in the same way as all other tracks. Only one automation lane is displayed by default. Reveal additional automation lanes by right-clicking over one of the automation lanes and choosing 'Show Additional Automation Lane'

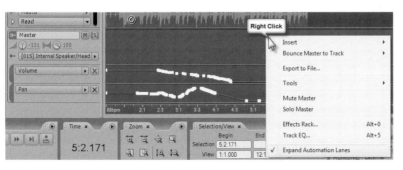

Creating a simple fade using automation in Adobe Audition

1 In the track panel place the track marker just before the point at which you want the fade to start.
2 In the mixer panel set the master track automation to 'Write'
3 Start the session playing
4 Use the mouse to draw the fader down to infinity
5 Stop the session

The automation state for the master track is now set to 'Touch'.

Automation can easily be edited simply by touching the control. The automation state for any track with automation is set to 'Touch' by default. Touch means that the automation will be edited if the fader is moved. To disable write, set the Automation state to 'Read'.

Clear edit points from any automation lane simply by expanding the lane, right clicking over the lane and choosing 'Clear Edit Points' from the menu. Alternatively, click on any edit handle and drag to any point on the track.

Choosing mastering effects

The master track is an opportunity to use effects which are required to process the entire mix. This may mean a very small amount of adjustment to the dynamic range using a compression plug in or adjustment to the stereo field using either the stereo widening effect or the stereo rotation effect. Use very high quality effects only at this stage. The master track is the final point for the data processed by Adobe Audition 2.0 before either becoming printed in the box or routed to an external device. Consider freezing as many tracks as possible to allow Adobe Audition as much processor power as necessary to process this final waveform.

Use subtle processes and effects at this point. For instance apply the stereo widening effect with 130 - 150% widening when a song reaches the chorus but drop back for the verses. Or deepen the stereo field with a large reverb and some additional widening just before the end of the song. Effects can be automated in exactly the same way as volume and pan. Alternatively, print your final stereo waveform with no effects and EQ at all. Import the master stereo waveform into the edit view and use the mastering rack to process the stereo waveform in isolation.

Automating the multitrack view

Automation is now a common tool for by the mix engineer. Automation enables the engineer to produce a complex mix inside the PC. Automation also saves the engineer time by removing the need to balance waveforms or deadhead clips as fader movements and mute toggles can be entirely automated. This means that the engineer is able to quickly import waveforms into the session then balance and mix using automation instead of having to pre-pare the waveforms in the edit view or use clip envelopes. Every control in the mixer panel can be automated along with most controls in the VST effects and controls from 3rd party VST effects. Bear in mind that automation increases processor load and may have an impact on the responsiveness of your computer depending on the resources available.

Methods of automation in Adobe Audition
Adobe Audition 2.0 enables mix automation in two ways:

• Clip envelopes
• Automation lanes

Clip envelopes produce simple volume or pan curves over just that clip. The volume or pan curves are not reproduced on the mixer panel. Clip envelopes are used to balance clip levels, for crossfading and for repetition, such as fading a phrase inside the clip.

Automation lanes contain mix information programmed in real time as the mix is playing. For instance fader movements are recorded into the volume lane when any track state is set to record. Automation lanes can also be edited if the handles are dragged with the mouse in the same way as dragging handles in clip envelopes.

Mixer automation is creating movements in mixer controls that are replayed with the session. Typically Mixer Automation is used for track length performance automation such as creating special effects using reverbs, stereo widening or fading effects in or out of the mix. Mixer automation is saved within the session and is rendered along with all other clip properties etc when the session is printed. Creating automated mixer controls means that complex mixes can be created within the box. The Adobe Audition mixer can have an unlimited number of tracks. Automated mixer hardware costs many thousands. Mixing inside the box with Adobe Audition 2.0 enables similar functionality, and the creation of comparable audio productions at a fraction of the price. This provides the Adobe Audition user with the ability to compete with A – Class studios.

Any control in the mixer panel can be automated. This includes sends and mute, solo, etc. Effect parameters including VST effects can also be auto-mated. The automation technique is the same for every control.

Automation states
Each track on the mixer can read or write automation independently in any one of four modes or 'states'. The tracks ability to read or write data depends on the automation state.

Live Session View

Off In this state automation for the track is completely disabled.

Read (default) Automation data for that track will be read while the track is playing.

Latch Overwrites automation data when you touch the control and continues to record until the track stops. For example when editing a fade; the fader will stay at infinity when you release the mouse button and the handle will stay at infinity until the track stops.

Touch Overwrites data with new data when the control is moved but does not overwrite data on untouched regions of the track. For example when editing a fade; the fader will stay at infinity until you release the mouse button. At this time the automation data will return to previous values while the track is playing.

Write Completely overwrites any automation data for that control on that track. Writes the current setting for the control when the track starts, without waiting for that control to change

Creating an automated control
1   Set the automation mode of any track to 'touch'
2   Start the session playback
3   Touch any control or button with the mouse

Automation lanes
Automation data is recorded in lanes underneath the clip in the track panel. Each control will record data into a new or different lane. This typically means that a single track can have many lanes. For this reason the automation lanes are hidden by default. From the right click menu in any track choose 'Expand Automation Lanes' The multitrack view will expand to show an additional lane under the currently selected track. Reveal additional lanes using the small + button in the track properties. Control movements are shown as 'handles' in just the same way as envelope data is drawn over clips. Handles can be dragged and moved in exactly the same way. Typically, large numbers of handles appear in the automation lanes causing difficulty when dragging handles to create curves etc. Overwrite automation data with new data rather than attempt to manage multiple handles.

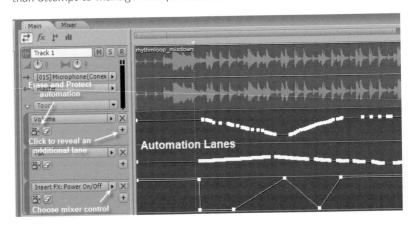

Use the erase tool on each automation lane to delete all data within that lane. Protect completed automation lanes with the padlock tool. Effects and EQ properties can also be protected against being over-written using the padlock control within each rack. In the effects panel the padlock control is a toggle for each effect, not overall for the entire rack. An additional control to globally pro-tect the entire rack is placed in the lower right hand corner of the rack.

Choose automation properties for each lane using the automation menu. Left click on the menu to produce a list of controls for that track. Controls which have saved automation data are indicated with a *.

Automation data cannot be copied like waveform data. Because of this, it is necessary to produce new curves wherever automation is required. Use clip envelopes if automation needs to be repeated over the track.

Tip

If you experience unexpected fading or boosting of track volumes just before recording, make sure that all automation states are set to off. Automation runs as soon as tracks are record enabled, before the transport starts. Always finish recording before applying automation and set automation to off for all track when in a recording situation.

Exporting your mix and creating a CD

The output of the mixer can be directed to any installed soundcard device for recording by an external program or CD burner, etc. Alternatively the mixer output can be rendered to a single stereo waveform inside the PC. This sin-gle waveform can be the source for a CD print or imported into another appli-cation such as Premiere Pro.

From the file menu choose Export, Audio Mix Down (Ctrl + Shift + Alt + M). The Export dialogue appears with the location of the last saved export in the main window.

Sessions exported to wav are always exported at the sample rate of the session although the bit depth can be adjusted. If the export is intended for an application or device that cannot handle high sample rates the export must be imported back into Adobe Audition and

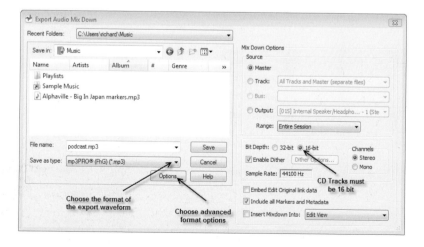

processed in the edit view where sample rate conversion will downsample the data (F11 to produce the convert sample rate dialogue). The option for Inserting the Mixdown into edit view in the Export dialogue can be used in this case.

The mixdown file can be used to produce a red book standard CD right from within Adobe Audition 2.0 without any further processing.

1   Import the mixdown into the File panel if it's not already there.
2   Switch to the CD view
3   In the CD view drag the mixdown onto the main panel
4   If necessary use track properties to change track name (CD Text)
5   Write the CD

During the write process the mixdown track is downsampled and filtered automatically. It's not necessary to downsample the exported track prior to writing to CD

Exporting wav files

Wav files are the highest quality. The wav file contains the track exactly as you heard it. If the export is not intended for CD, the wav file can be exported with exactly the same resolution (24, or 32 bit and 48 or 96kHz rate) as the Adobe Audition session. Multimedia presentations, film soundtracks or game soundtracks will sound just as good as the original session.

Preparing mp3 files for export

If your export is intended for low resolution distribution such as digital distribution or Podcast choose the option for mp3 in the 'Files of Type; field from within the Export dialogue. Click over 'Options' to see additional options. The options dialogue includes various options depending on the destination of the mp3 and should be used with care as they all have an effect on the quality of the mp3

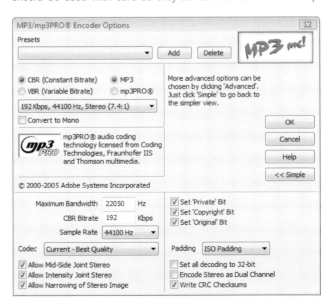

encoding. Always the intention is to produce as high quality sound as possible in the smallest possible file size. These advanced options enable different mp3 and mp3PRO options which are used in combination to achieve this.

When encoding mp3 files, keep in mind the nature of the decoder. For instance if your file contains speech intended for transmission to a mobile phone you will create a smaller file if you choose to encode in mono. Additionally encoding the file with mp3PRO data will recreate missing high frequencies at very low bit rate. However if the decoder cannot decode mp3PRO data the playback quality will be badly affected. Be careful if deciding on encoding data as mp3PRO as very few software decoders and no hardware decoders currently support this standard. However mp3PRO is used in Internet Radio and telephony.

Variable Bit Rate encoding should only be used if you are sure of where your mp3 file may be decoded as not all mp3 players can decode VBR files.

The complexity and nuance of mp3 encoding is a book in itself. Adobe Audition 2.0 presents a number of mp3 presets which take some of the guesswork out of encoding mp3 audio for general distribution. Above all, encoding an mp3 file incorrectly will turn your efforts into a waste of time – because you won't be sure that every decoder will be able to reproduce your data as you expect.

The following table lists four of the most popular mp3 presets, the most suitable application and the file size resulting from the encoding. The source file was a 16/44 stereo wave of 4mins 44secs. (49,051KB)

Decoder	Preset	Resulting File Size
PC or Mac software or mp3 player (iPod, iTunes Winamp etc.)	128kbps (Internet)	4450KB
Export to Premiere or other multimedia app for production	256kbps	8900KB
Podcasting (speech) or telephony	32kbps for voice (PRO)	1113KB
Internet or IP 'Radio Station' with dedicated decoder	pro VBR highest quality (PRO)	4398KB

Adobe Audition 2.0 decodes mp3 files and renders them as raw data with no further decoding required. However, this doesn't mean that the file is high quality again, just that the decoding isn't happening in real time. Encoding a decoded mp3 back to mp3 again introduces further noise that wouldn't have been apparent in the source and won't result in smaller file sizes/higher quality.

Preparing other file types for export

The default file type for uncompressed audio in the PC platform is Microsoft Windows PCM. However Adobe Audition 2.0 is able to create files for almost any platform. The following table lists the major file formats supported in the program.

Tip

Streaming audio requires a tricky combination of both quality and speed.

Settings for Streaming Audio; CBR, Mp3 (not PRO) 96kbps, 44100Hz, Max Bandwidth 22050 CBR 96kbps.

64 Bit Doubles	*.dbl	8 Byte doubles in Binary Form
8-Bit Signed	*.sam	MOD compatible format (22050Hz)
Amu-Law Wave	*.wav	Telephony only (CCITT standard G.711)

ACM Waveform	*.wav	Microsoft Audio Compression Manager
Amiga IFF-8SVX	*.iff *.svx	Commodore Amiga 8 Bit Mono
Apple AIFF	*.aif *.snd	Macintosh compatible
ASCII Text Data	*.txt	Standard Text Format
Audition Loop	*.cel	Loop file in enhanced MP3 format
Creative Sound Blaster	*.voc	Creative Labs Sound Blaster software
Dialogic ADPCM	*.vox	Telephony only (no header)
Diamondware Digitized	*.dwd	Game sound designers format
DVI/IMA ADPCM	*.wav	International Multimedia Association alternative to Microsoft ADPCM
Microsoft ADPCM	*.wav	Microsoft compressed audio
MPEG 3 (FhG)	*.mp3	Popular distribution form
Next/Sun	*.au *.snd	NeXT/Sun format used in Java apps
SampleVision	*.smp	Turtle Beach Samplevison
Windows PCM	*.wav	Default
PCM Raw Data	*.pcm *.raw	Raw data (unknown format)

The help file contains detailed scientific information about these formats and the ways in which Adobe Audition interacts with other software through them.

Third party lossless compression

The functionality of Adobe Audition can be extended with the use of third party utilities. Lossless compression programs enable you to distribute smaller files with no loss of quality.

Wavpack is regarded as the most developed of the 3rd party compression programs available. Wavpack provides lossless compression for Adobe Audition and other audio softwar e and hardware. Once encoded as Wavpack , the file can be unencoded and read by any audio application in the original format. The Wavpack program is available as a free download; www.wavpack.com

FLAC (Free Lossless Audio Codec) is a third party filter which is used inside Adobe Audition. The filter needs to be downloaded and copied to the Adobe Audition program directory. After copying the filter will appear in the list of options in the Save As Type menu. FLAC is regularly updated by the developer. http://www.vuplayer.com/audition.php

iTunes and MPEG-4

Files intended for use in iTunes, an iPod or an iPhone must be encoded as linear MPEG-4 (based on Apple's Quicktime) and given one of the following file extensions;

Audio Only	.m4a
MPEG-4 containing DRM information	.m4p
Podcasts and Audiobook	.m4b
Audio and Video combined	.mp4 and .m4v
Audio intended for Mobile Phone	.3gp and .3g2

A filter that enables opening of MPEG-4 format files (iTunes) is available from http://www.vuplayer.com/audition.php.

To save music for iTunes you need to first export the waveform in mp3 standard and then use the iTunes player to import the mp3 to your iTunes library.

Dolby Pro Logic surround sound

Sessions in the multitrack view can be encoded for 5.1 surround sound. The ability to produce 5.1 multichannel audio mixes 'in the box' means Adobe Audition 2.0 becomes the perfect partner for Premiere Pro and other video editing tools.

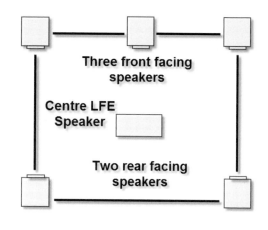

Surround sound is the term given to audio mixes that appear to surround the listener with sound. A traditional stereo mix is produced by two speakers (2 mix) sometimes supplemented with a mono LFE (Low Frequency Effects) subwoofer. This arrangement is called a 2.1 system as it includes two speakers with a single subwoofer. The professional 5.1 system includes 5 full range speakers and a LFE speaker. To comply with the Dolby specification the speakers should be placed in a room as follows; Three speakers in front of the listener. Two speakers behind the listener. One LFE in the centre, either behind the screen in a theatre or under the TV in a home cinema environment. This arrangement of devices provides a sensual environment for the listener, particularly when loud explosions go off under their seat!

Speaker placement for 5.1 Channel Surround (Analog Matrixed: Dolby Pro Logic 2). The source for this placement is a specially encoded stereo source such as the Adobe Audition surround sound encoder.

- Two front channel speakers; Left (L) and Right (R)
- One centre channel speaker at front (C)
- Two surround sound speakers at the rear; Left (LS) and Right (RS)
- Low frequency effects channel speaker (LFE)

All commercial movie DVD's and some commercial audio CD's have a soundtrack in this format. A decoder is required to hear the 5.1 surround sound effect.

Encoding a stereo source for 5.1 within Adobe Audition

The multitrack session does not need to be exported for the 5.1 encoding. This is important as the multitrack session mix will need to be rebalanced for 5.1. A copy of the session containing elements suitable for 5.1 should be saved as a different session name.

From within the multitrack view choose Surround Encoder from the View menu. The Surround Encoder options appears in a new window. This is not a panel and (unfortunately) can't be docked.

Tracks in the session are arranged on the left of the surround sound encoder. If any of the session tracks are muted they will appear in the

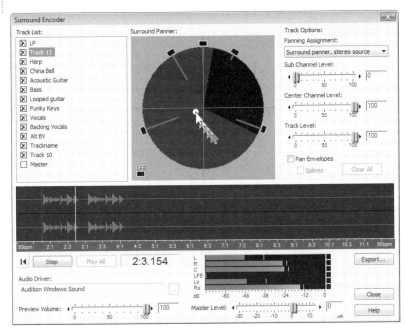

encoder but won't be heard. Add or remove tracks from the encoder by removing the check marks on the left of each track name. Below the track list is the master track. This isn't enabled by default as usually the individual tracks are encoded. However, just the master track can be selected if a very simple encoding is all that is needed.

Each of the tracks in the list has its own pan properties. In other words the Harp track in my session is given its own panning curve, so is the China Bell track etc.

1　Click on one of the tracks to see the waveform in the graph.
2　Choose a Panning Assignment, a default stereo source or a simple mono right left pan, etc. for that track.
3　Preview the assignment using the controls at the bottom of the dialogue.

When the stereo source assignment is used, the panning assignment can be made by grabbing the white dot in the centre of the screen and moving it around the graph. Animated depictions of the speaker range will show how the listener will hear the surround sound at that point. The white dot is not the listener. The white dot represents the focus of the panning assignment. The listener is always assumed to be in the centre of the sound stage, at the point where the X and Y crosshairs meet.

Below the Surround Panner graph is the waveform. Just like the session, the waveform has a yellow start position marker. The white dot on the Surround Panner graph indicates the position in space at the point in time indicated by the yellow start position marker.

This is best illustrated if the option to show pan envelopes is selected. Select Pan Envelopes and also select Spline Envelopes. The graph now shows two lines across the waveform. The green line is left/right movement and the

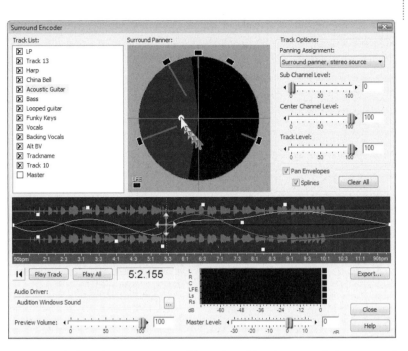

yellow line is front/rear movement. Move the white dot around the surround panner to see the relationship between the front/rear and left right speakers.

It's becoming clear now how very complex mixes can be encoded with the Surround Encoder tool. Even more exciting is how to automate these movements, to have a tank move across the room, or a spaceship fly over your head.

Automation is achieved by placing handles along the waveform. The Surround Panner will indicate the movement of the stereo field as the yellow start position marker moves along the waveform. Underneath the waveform graph is a small moving graph showing amplitudes in each area of the stage. Extreme panning can easily move amplitude above the clipping point, use the master fader if necessary to trim audio.

When the encoding is complete, click

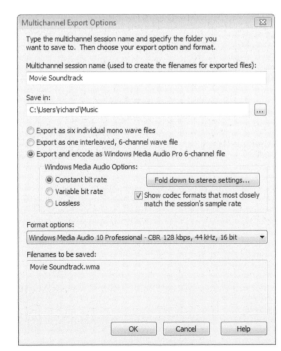

over the Export button to see the Export Options dialogue.   Adobe Audition 2.0 currently has filters for Windows Media Audio only. Encode the sound-track as a 6 channel file.

The edit view

The edit view is a workbench on which stereo or mono waveforms can be examined, processed and exported both quickly and accurately.

Within the edit view the waveform can be shaped and prepared for any use from video soundtrack to a ring tone for a cell phone. This is because the edit view allows you to see the waveform as an amplitude shape, by frequency or by pan. Effects and processes are applied to the waveform in any of these modes. Through careful selection and application of processes the raw waveform can be shaped and finished until it is suitable for export or import into the multitrack view. Because processes in the edit view are applied individually there is no limit on the number of effects that can be used.

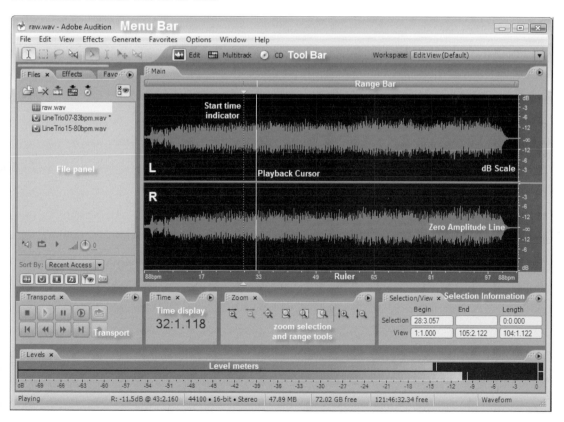

Differences between effects in multitrack and edit view

Although both the edit view and the multitrack enable processing of waveforms, within the edit view changes made to waveforms are destructive. Adobe Audition provides numerous levels of undo but changes to the waveform must be saved before the program is closed. Effects and other processes are then saved to the waveform. In the multitrack view effects and processes are made to the session instead of the waveform. This is a non-destructive process because the underlying waveforms are not changed by the application of effects, EQ and balance etc. The edit view cannot play more than one mono or stereo waveform at one time.

Edit view basics

The edit view, Multitrack view and CD view share the same files panel. Drag files from the files panel into the edit view or open new waveforms using File, Open in exactly the same way as you would open any Windows document. Press play on the spacebar or use the mouse to press play on the transport. The yellow track position marker will move over the waveform and audio will be heard.

Edit view audio preferences

If nothing is heard as the track position cursor moves across the waveform (and if the level meters are moving), check the assignment for the edit view in hardware preferences. Edit view and multitrack view audio settings are discrete in Adobe Audition 2.0. Audio from the edit view can be diverted to a different set of outputs or even to a different audio driver. To see Audio the Audio Preferences dialogue choose Edit, Audio Hardware Setup. From within audio preferences choose the ASIO or the Audition Windows Sound (WDM) driver and the input and output pair for the edit view. If possible use ASIO drivers. WDM drivers are not optimised for Adobe Audition.

It is also necessary to set the correct Input Assignment when recording into the edit view as Adobe Audition will choose the first available device as the default for the edit view. Even though Adobe Audition 2.0 supports ASIO, it is not possible to use Audition Mix in the edit view and only external monitoring is available.

As with all the common dialogue boxes in Adobe Audition, files can be previewed before opening using the Autoplay feature. Open files are placed in the file panel but only one waveform can be played in the edit view at a time. When multiple files are opened in the edit view the file at the top of the list is the one currently loaded into the edit view workspace. Files can also be chosen from the Windows menu. Files with changes not yet saved are identified with an asterisk (*).

Open Append

Open multiple files in one edit view panel by choosing File>Open Append from the File menu. Open Append causes Adobe Audition to insert another file at the very end of the currently open file. A marker range is automatically created for each file.

This feature can be used to compile CD's for printing inside Adobe

Audition. Change the marker type for each range to 'Track' and drag each track range into the main panel within the CD view.

By default the new waveform is scaled to fit inside the current window. Stereo waveforms are laid left to right with the left side of the waveform lying above the right side of the waveform. Mono waveforms are placed in the centre of the view. Above the waveform is the marker bar and the horizontal range bar. Below the waveform is the ruler. The region at the far right of the waveform is calibrated in db from infinity to 0dBfs (DeciBel Full Scale). The point at which the zero amplitude line meets the scale is the lowest sample value or infinity. Right click on the scale to choose alternative view options such as viewing in percentage or samples. Choose the default db scale for general audio editing. Choose zoom full to reset the scale to the default.

Click and drag the edges of the horizontal range bar to zoom in and out of the waveform. Use Alt+= and Alt+- to zoom in vertically. Additional range options are revealed by right clicking on the range bar.

Tip

Files may not open in the order chosen in the Open Append dialogue. For instance four files named 1.wav, 2.wav, 3.wav and 4.wav may open in the order 1,4,2,3. Open the files in the correct order by using shift and click. Select 4.wav, press and hold the shift key while clicking on 1.wav. Files will open in the correct order.

Edit view transport

Transport functions are the same in the edit view and multitrack view. However the record button has different right click options depending on the view. Loop while recording is not available in the edit view and is replaced instead with the timed record feature. There is also an option to disable the record function altogether. Right Click over the record button to see these options.

Tip

Timed Recording prevents the transport from recording until a certain time period has elapsed. Create a new waveform and choose timed record mode from the Options menu or from the record button right click menu. Start recording. Adobe Audition will present the timed record mode options for recording length, date and time.

If you haven't already done so, now is the time to enable VST and Direct X effects. Choose Effects, Add Remove VST Directory and Enable Direct X Effects . VST effects won't be visible in the Effects menu until this is done.

Scrubbing and spooling over the edit view

Audio can be scrubbed over the yellow track position marker. This enabled precise positioning of markers and ranges without the guesswork involved in visually placing markers on the waveform

The scrubbing tool

1 Zoom in on the area of the waveform where the marker needs to be positioned.

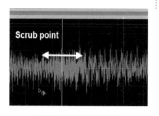

Scrub point

Tip

Use ctrl+scrub and shift+scrub for additional scrubbing options.

2 Select the scrubbing tool from the tool bar
3 Click once on the waveform to position the yellow start position maker
4 While holding the left button down, drag the tool forwards or backwards along the waveform. A white playback ruler will indicate the point at which the waveform is playing.
5 When you release the left button the yellow start position marker will jump to the last point of the white playback ruler.

Recording directly into the edit view

Connect a suitable stereo source to the input of your soundcard.

Press F10 to test levels coming into Adobe Audition. The level meters should move in time with your music and should have a max amplitude of around -8 to -9 dBfs

Levels peaking at -9dB

| -39 | -36 | -33 | -30 | -27 | -24 | -21 | -18 | -15 | -12 | -9 | -6 | -3 | 0 |

| R: -inf dB @ 1:1.000 | 96000 • 16-bit • Stereo | 71.80 GB free | 55:46:19.28 free | Waveform |

Press record on the transport bar (Ctrl+Record). The New Waveform dialogue box will appear and prompt for a sample rate for the new waveform. Choose a sample rate appropriate to the project and click OK.

The waveform will scroll across the screen as it records. Press spacebar to stop. Adobe Audition will auto select the entire

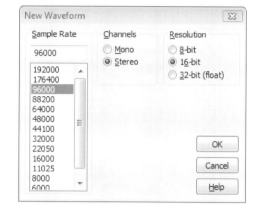

waveform as a range ready for further processing. Press the spacebar or use the mouse to press the play button on the transport to hear the playback.

Tip

Basic soundcards without complex routing won't be able to route sound to speakers or headphones while recording in the edit view. This is because only external monitoring is enabled in the edit view. To hear the source while recording you'll need an external mixer to route the source to both headphones and Adobe Audition. No additional equipment is needed if using imported waveforms or when simply playing back.

Essential processing within the edit view

The rest of this section assumes that you don't have the facilities of a world class recording environment (and why not? This is world class recording kit after all?). Without specialist environmental conditions your waveform will certainly require some topping and tailing, balancing and some elementary EQ. After that - it's just a question of mixing.

Waveform analysis

Zoom in vertically to the waveform using the Alt+ = keystroke to bring the maximum amplitude of the waveform to the top of the scale. Drag the edge of the range bar inwards to zoom in. Drag the range bar along the horizontal track to meet the yellow start time indicator.

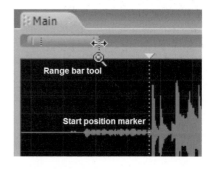

If your input levels are OK, the recorded waveform should peak well below -3dBfs. This allows for the headroom needed by effects processes and for transients. A transient is a very fast peak which is too fast for the meters to catch. They are often caused by loud high frequency sources such as cymbals or even by breath or tongue sounds. It's necessary to allow for the presence of transients in the recording by setting levels at the point of maximum signal to noise but still allowing at least 6db of headroom.

Waveforms recorded with insufficient control over level can either clip or be too quiet. Clipping occurs when the level present at the input of the soundcard exceeds the ability of the soundcard to literally process the numbers required to translate that analogue voltage into digital data. At extreme levels the soundcard will simply give up trying and produce nothing at all. Lower levels will cause the soundcard to produce garbage which is seen as amplitude data at maximum amplitude (0dBfs). Sound recorded like this is unusable as no meaningful data exists in the clipped information. Unfortunately this means re-recording the waveform from scratch. So don't book that orchestra until you've got a handle on your input levels!

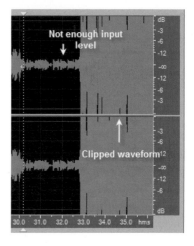

Levels coming into the soundcard that are too quiet produce very small numbers which translate into low amplitude waveforms. In this case the information that you need exists within the waveform but is mixed up with the other garbage that is in the recording environment (air conditioning, people sounds, ambient noise, etc.) Data recorded in this way will never be high quality but usually can be rescued, at least to the point where it can be understood as music or speech etc. Simply raising the levels of the waveform as a whole doesn't solve this problem as simple amplification will simply amplify the background noise at the same rate as the sound you need to keep. A more complex (but still easy within Adobe Audition 2.0) procedure called restoration is required to make some sense of the waveform.

Markers in the edit view

Markers can be placed over the waveform in the Edit View. These are used either to identify precise points in the waveform or, in the case of a range marker, to identify sections of the waveform. Processes such as envelopes can then be applied within the selected range. If ranges are not set the effect or process is applied over the entire waveform. The key to successful audio editing in Adobe Audition lies in accurate positioning and using of markers.

Placing markers

Markers are used inside the edit view in exactly the same way as in the mul-

---

Tip

Input levels are like the Three Bears; not too loud, not too quiet, just right at around -9dBfs.

titrack view, Use F8 at any time to place a marker and view markers in the marker window. Left click and drag select a range over any part of the waveform and press F8 to create a range marker. Markers can be renamed and marker types can be changed. The default marker type is the Cue Marker. Delete markers by right clicking on the blue marker triangle above the waveform. Alternatively delete markers in the Marker Window. Move markers by left clicking and dragging the marker along the track.

Marker shortcuts in the edit view

Rgn	F8	Creates cue or range over selection
Trk	Shift + F8	Inserts track marker for use in the CD Burning dialog
Idx	Ctrl + F8	Inserts index marker

The Marker Window

Markers appear as blue vertical lines in over the waveform. Use Edit, Snapping, Snap to Markers to accurately place the yellow start position marker over any marker. The marker is one sample in width. A list of markers and their names, types etc. is available in the Marker List (Alt + 8). The following functions are also available from this Window.

Autoplay

Within the Markers window click on any range to hear.

Add Marker

Adds a new default marker type at the position of the start position pointer.

Delete

Deletes the selected marker or range.

Merge

Merges two or more markers to form a range.

Batch Process Marker Regions

Exports marker ranges as files. Use the marker label as a filename or use a single name (eg; song) and append with a number. The contents of each range will be exported as a file with each new file having a different name (song1,song2,song3,etc).

Alternatively use the create silence function to automatically insert a small period of silence before each marker. If used to process marker ranges silence will only be created before the first marker in the range.

Placing markers automatically on beats or over phrases

Drag Select over an area of the waveform that contains the phrase and choose from the following menu items.

Adjust Selection To Phrase

If a range has been selected over an area of speech, this option will adjust the boundaries of the highlighted area inwards after and before digital silence

Find Phrases and Mark

Adobe Audition will look for the points of lowest amplitude within the selected area and create a cue range from this. Although the menu item is called 'Find Phrases And Mark' this feature will only create one cue range even if two or three distinct phrases are within the selected area.

Find Beats and Mark

To detect each phrase automatically choose 'Find Beats and Mark'. This feature causes the program to scan the waveform and place a cue marker at the front of each phrase. However, it doesnít join the markers to create ranges. To do this, open the Cue Window and shift-click or ctrl-click two or more items in the Cue List. With more than one cue highlighted the 'Merge' button will become available. Press the merge button to create a range from two cues. Add Labels and Descriptions to the cue range as usual.

Auto-Mark Settings

Define silence and audio in this dialog so Auto-Cue can make decisions regarding which areas in the waveform are speech or not. If the waveform is well recorded the definition of silence can be set very low to around -80dB. However if the waveform contains background noise the threshold must be raised to around -34dB or so depending on the amplitude and frequency the background noise. If words and phrases are skipped or removed raise or lower these values accordingly. Use the Find Levels function to scan the waveform and estimate thresholds automatically.

Trim Digital Silence

When the lower threshold has been calculated correctly this function will remove any areas below the lower threshold and defined as digital silence.

This feature is incredibly useful for removing 'dead space' in a commercial radio production such as an advert. By removing small areas of silence the voice over can contain more content in the same time period, valuable when inserting sections such as terms and conditions.

Autodetection of peaks (beats) inside the waveform

The Find Beats feature is used to find peaks in the waveform that exceed adjustable values. From the Edit menu choose 'Find Beats' Use Shift + [or Shift +] to detect peaks before or after the start position pointer. The pointer will move to the position of the detected beat.

Adobe Audition can detect beats (drum hits or other fast peaks) within a waveform and place markers at each hit. This feature can be used to segment a drum loop and produce (for instance) eight one crotchet beat segments.

- Open a waveform containing a short rhythmic selection. The selection shouldn't contain transients or other peaks such as a rhythmic crash or

ride cymbal and ideally would contain just kick, bass and snare.
• From the Edit menu choose Find Beats and Mark
• Leave the settings at their default and press OK

Adobe Audition will place a new marker at each point in the waveform that exceeds the values in the 'Find Beats' dialogue. Open the Markers Window (Alt + 8) and merge markers to produce ranges. The same technique can be used to identify phrases, such as sections of speech or music, in a waveform.

Truncating waveforms

With markers in place it's now possible to apply selective processing over parts of the waveform. The first process is usually 'deadheading' the waveform to remove empty space at the beginning and end. This allows you to remove noise, lower the demand on the processor when the waveform is imported into the multitrack view and to save storage space. Even empty space in a waveform is data which has to be processed.

• Place the start position maker close to the start of the recorded sound in the waveform
• Use the Zoom To Selection tool to zoom in to the marker until the waveform appears clearly.
• Drag select left from the start position marker right to the left edge of the waveform
• Press the delete key on the keyboard

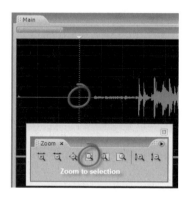

The waveform will move left as the unwanted portion of the waveform is removed. Repeat the process on the end of the waveform. Be careful that you don't clip the end of any trailing notes or fades. Drag select a range at the end of the waveform and press the spacebar to hear just that portion of the wave. Leave at least 1 second of space after the very end of any trailing notes to ensure that no data is lost.

Using envelopes inside the waveform

Envelopes are amplitude curves applied at the beginning, end or over the entire waveform. Envelopes can be used to create a smooth fade in for the audio, a long smooth fade out or creatively such as fractionally raising the amplitude of certain sections of a performance. If an envelope is applied to the start and end of the waveform, the empty space before and after the lowest part of the envelope can be permanently removed.

In Adobe Audition 2.0 envelopes are applied over clips in the multitrack view or to the source waveform. Although applying envelopes to the waveform will change the data, this is an option which can be considered in a complex session or when you can be confident that the envelope will always be applied.

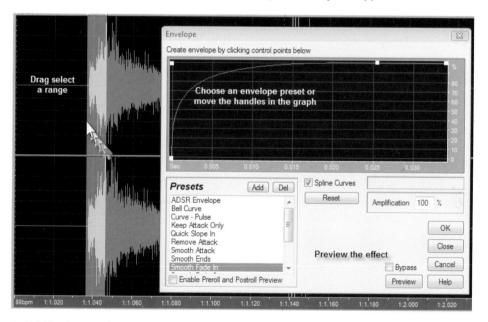

1 Within the waveform drag select a range at the front of the waveform over which the envelope is to be applied.
2 Choose Effects,Amplitude, Envelope(process)from the menu bar
3 Choose a preset or move the handles in the graph.
4 Press OK

Envelopes used at the beginning and ends of waveforms can have a surprising effect on the session. The impression of space and depth is greater, particularly in conversational speech.

Normalising and amplifying waveforms

The amplitude of the prepared waveform can now be adjusted. At this point we are not looking to affect the way that the waveform sounds, or to change the way people listen to the waveform. Normalising is simply a way to make sure that all the waveforms in a session or in a group of waveforms achieve standard amplitude. Group waveform normalising can also be used if a number of waveforms need to be adjusted at the same time.

Normalising

Normalising is a process effect which is used to raise the amplitude of a waveform by a certain amount relative to the difference between the maximum amplitude of the highest peak in the waveform and the top of the scale (0dBfs). For instance, a waveform has a peak amplitude of -15dB. After normalising, every sample in the waveform will be amplified by 15dB (if during normalising, the process was set to amplify by 100%). Normalising provides a very quick way of amplifying waveforms without the risk of clipping the highest point of the waveform. It is a simple away of normalising a waveform in relation to other waveforms but should not be confused with dynamic processes such as Compression which reduce dynamic range to make quiet sounds louder in relation to loud sounds. If you have a group of waveforms created during the same session then use the group normalise tool.

Process EQ using the parametric equaliser in the spectral view

Waveforms that have not been recorded in an acoustically controlled environment will require some form of remedial correction to remove resonant peaks and troublesome frequencies. Use the parametric processor to correct this kind of issue. It's not possible to completely resolve EQ problems with the parametric equaliser alone. In the same way, parametric EQ won't change the nature of the waveform aside from boosting or cutting frequencies. Changing the fundamental sound of the wave, such as taking a waveform recorded in a room, and turning it into the sound of a waveform created in a cathedral requires other processes such as modelling software.

Within Adobe Audition 2.0 the spectral frequency display produces a 3D visual image of the concentration of frequencies within the waveform, plotted over the spectrum over time. Although EQ correction can easily be made when using the waveform view, the Spectral Display View is the best environment for remedial correction and balancing of EQ within the waveform.

Bear in mind that parametric EQ is a destructive process involving attenuating (cutting or turning down) and boosting frequencies. Each frequency has a relationship with other frequencies over time within the waveform and a different relationship when that waveform is used alongside other waveforms in a session. The bottom line then, is less is more. No more than 3dB of correction should be used in either direction (up or down) for general (not critical) correction. If you find that you need to use more than 3dB of correction consider recording the waveform again or examine the listening environment.

The spectral view

Frequency selective processes such as audio restoration are much easier using the Adobe Audition 2.0 Spectral View. In the spectral view the amplitude waveform is replaced with a spectral waveform plotting frequency rather than amplitude over time. Produce the spectral view with Shift+F.

Info

Phase and Pan spectral views are disabled for mono waveforms.

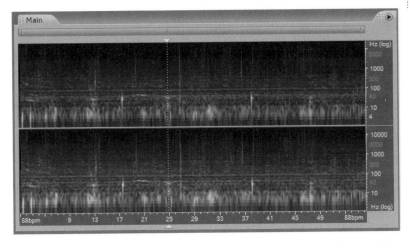

Tip

Right click over the scale at the right of the display to change the view from linear to logarithmic. The logarithmic scale is aligned to human hearing and to the dB which is also a logarithmic unit.

The edit view spectral frequency display produces a graphic display of frequency over time. In the spectral display frequencies are plotted on the y-axis with lower frequencies towards the zero amplitude line. Time is plotted on the x-axis. The concentration or energy of frequency is shown as colour with brighter colours indicating more energy at that point. Troublesome frequencies can be identified by their colour and position on the display.

Open the waveform and switch to Spectral Display (Shift-F). Spectral Display preferences enable different colour options. Choose Window, spectral controls to see colour preferences and choose a suitable high contrast colour scheme or, if you have the inclination drag the brilliance controls around the Spectral Controls dialogue and create your own scheme. The spectral display is laid out with 0dBfs and brighter colours at the right of the scale. Drag the markers around to enhance certain amplitudes over others.

Certain areas within the Spectral Display will be brighter than others. These bright areas are loud frequencies.

Adobe Audition 2.0 enables frequency specific selection of parts of the waveform in the edit view. This is called Frequency Space Editing. The workflow is almost exactly the same as selecting areas of the waveform in the default Waveform Display. However unlike the Waveform display, in the Spectral Display the selection can be made over a small portion of the waveform – not a slice from top to bottom. Effects and processes are then applied only to that selection. This enables extremely precise audio restoration.

A choice of three selection tools is provided in the edit view;

- The Time Tool, S
- The Lasso Tool, L
- The Marquee Tool, M

The fourth tool is the Scrub tool used for hearing a small section of the track when identifying key points such as the beginning of phrases. Drag the scrub tool over the waveform. The lasso and marquee tools are only available in the spectral frequency view.

Removing noise from a waveform using frequency range display

This waveform contains just two sine wave tones; one at 900 Hz and one at 440 Hz. In the area selected with the selection tool a notch filter process was applied. The notch filter was set to grossly attenuate (to -80dB) a very narrow band of frequencies centred around 900 Hz. Frequency range display

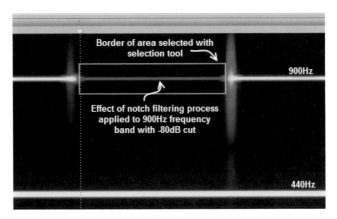

allowed the process over just the 900Hz frequency band leaving the 440Hz tone completely untouched.

The same workflow can be used to remove frequency bands from recordings. In this recording there is a difficult hum created by a nearby refrigerator. The hum is centred around 100Hz but annoyingly lies very close to a low voice that we needed to preserve.

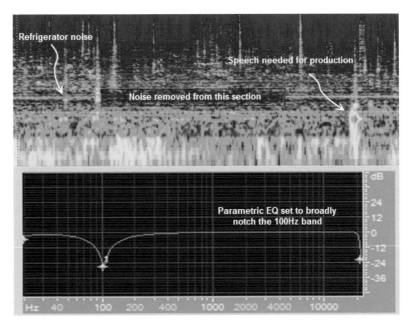

1   Zoom in to the area of the frequencies that require attention
2   Use the selection tool to select the Frequency Range Display

3 Use the parametric equaliser to first identify and then attenuate the troublesome band and also to set a Q range that will not destroy other frequencies.

This would not have been possible in the edit view. The Parametric EQ could only have been applied to all frequencies and amplitudes in one time 'slice' inside the waveform. The 100Hz filter would have affected a much greater range of frequencies and the effect would have been much more visible.

Marquee tool

The marquee tool is used for Frequency Range Display in the same way as the selection tool. The marquee too is a much finer tool which can be used to select audio 'shapes' within the waveform for processing. Select the marquee tool draw around sections of the spectral view. Expand selections by holding the ctrl key while widening the selection.

Tip

In practice the selection tool is useful for selecting frequency bands across the entire waveform while the marquee tool is useful for precise removal and audio restoration. Overuse of Frequency Range Selection can produce unnatural frequency shifts within the audio. Apply less power within process effects when using this technique.

Time tool

The time tool offers no advantages within the Spectral View as it is only able to produce time slices rather than discrete selections of the frequency band. However it is useful to use the spectral display when trimming waveforms as low high frequencies typically the result of a long fade are easier to identify and avoid in the spectral view.

Edit view display modes

The edit view has four display modes;

Waveform View	Shift + W	Amplitude over time
Spectral Frequency View	Shift + F	Frequency distribution with amplitude
Spectral Pan	Shift + A	Stereo information over time
Spectral Phase	Shift + E	Phase information over time

Waveform view is the default 2D view plotting amplitude over time. Within the Waveform View amplitudes are displayed as peaks. This provides immediate information for waveforms that may contain clipped data but it contains little frequency information. On the other hand this view loads immediately and requires the least resources from the host computer.

Spectral frequency view is a long term feature of Adobe Audition. The Spectral view provides information on frequency over time with additional amplitude data shown as colour changes. This is the most detailed waveform view and therefore the most useful particularly for audio restoration processing where the effect of a process can easily be limited to a set of frequencies without affecting other frequencies at all.

The spectral pan view provides spectral panorama and amplitude information over time. Amplitude data is spread over 180degrees with sounds panned hard right at the most extreme setting of 180 degrees. Sounds panned centrally appear at 90 degrees or the centre line. Louder sounds have brighter colours. The Spectral Pan view is most useful when compared with the Spectral Phase view for analysis of production waveforms where unbalanced mixes can be disguised by effects etc.

The spectral phase view is used to visualise parts of the waveform that are out of 'phase'. Out of phase waveforms amplify or attenuate frequencies depending on the polarity of the waveform or the degree of phase cancellation. Phase cancellation is a problem as frequencies may be unnaturally affected at different times. This effect can be heard if a white or pink noise is processed using the Delay, Phase Shift effect. Phase cancellation can also be used as a tool. For instance phase cancellation is often used in microphone arrays and in Mid-Side recording.

Info

The dictionary definition of Phase (see http://www.mixguides.com) is the 'relative measurement referenced to the start point of a cycle of a periodic waveform'. In simple terms this means the distance from any point along the wave cycle to the point at which the cycle ends. A tone of 440Hz is a vibration of 440 cycles per second. Each complete vibration is a cycle containing an excursion of 180 degrees positive and 180 degrees negative. Phase is the starting point of that cycle. Phase cancellation is the attenuation that occurs when two waveforms which have the same frequency are combined.

Colour preferences for the Spectral view can be set within the Spectral Controls panel (Window, Spectral Controls) Bands of colour are created for amplitude ranges which are then used to clarify the Spectral View. For instance the Scan Bar preset is useful within the Spectral Pan view when visualising brightness peaks in the waveform. Alternatively use the Topographic preset in the Spectral Phase view to provide a high contrast image of the waveform.

Correcting phase problems using the spectral phase display

Phase problems are introduced by incorrectly wired equipment, poorly developed processes or simple frequency shifting. A small amount of phase cancellation is normal in every waveform and shouldn't be a cause for overdue concern.

The pics opposite show two recordings made around 40 years apart. The Beatles *Eleanor Rigby* was recorded in 1966 using state of the art equipment in scientific surroundings at EMI's studios by highly skilled engineers and technicians. This short section of *Eleanor Rigby* reveals considerable phase mis-alignments, probably introduced at the recording stage.

Phase analysis of David Gray's 2002 recording *Be Mine* reveals little or no phase travel. The recording technique and the equipment used have produced a recording which is almost technically perfect from this perspective.

The point of this is not to compare the music of The Beatles with the music of David Gray. But to show that two complex multitrack recordings, each successful in their own right, have two entirely different phase fingerprints and neither of these detracts from the music at all.

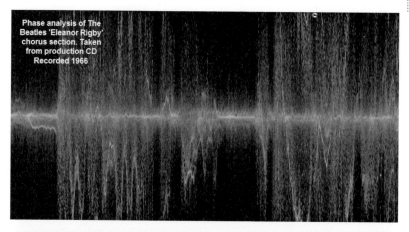

Phase analysis of The Beatles 'Eleanor Rigby' chorus section. Taken from production CD Recorded 1966

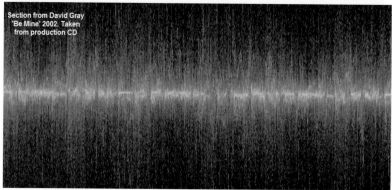

Section from David Gray 'Be Mine' 2002. Taken from production CD

Phase correction in the edit view

This section of a stereo backing vocal part was mistakenly recorded with one microphone 180 degrees out of phase. The resulting phase analysis reveals that all of the amplitude information is 180 degrees out of phase. If this backing track is played back in stereo the vocals are heard. However if the track is summed to mono, the phase cancellation effect completely removes all of the backing vocals. The phase can be corrected by inverting one side of the stereo waveform only.

- In the edit view choose the normal waveform display.
- Drag select over the left channel only
- With the left channel selected choose Effects, Invert from the menu bar

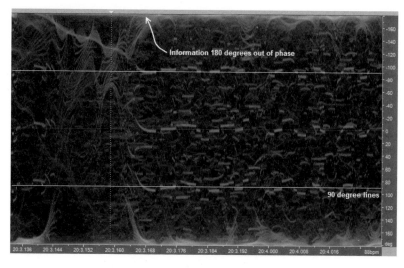

Information 180 degrees out of phase

90 degree lines

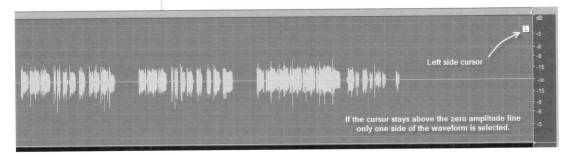

Left side cursor

If the cursor stays above the zero amplitude line
only one side of the waveform is selected.

The Invert process mirrors the phase information in the selected area. The effect is to reverse the phase of the left channel and so remove phase cancellation.

Spectral pan display

The Spectral Pan display plots amplitude over time with panorama (left / right) information on the X axis and time display on the Y axis. Louder amplitudes have brighter colours in the display. Information in the display doesn't become meaningful until a only a small region of the waveform is shown, at which point the panorama details become apparent. Display of pan over time is useful if accurate information regarding the positioning of a waveform in the panorama is required.

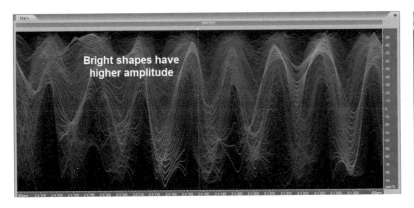

Bright shapes have
higher amplitude

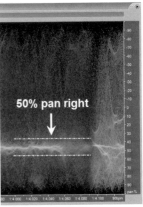

50% pan right

Parts of the waveform on the right have been panned too wide in an export. The wide pan parts are shown as a high contrast line in the lower half of the display. The effect of this is a sudden shift to the right. This is an issue for radio and TV. When listening to a broadcast the listener location is usually to the right or left of the stage (a listener sitting in the driving seat of a car will never get the true stereo image). Dramatic pan effects translate into lowering or boosting of the level for that particular part. Networked R&B and Rap productions where vocal clarity is crucial are always panned central with very little information in the extremes of the panorama field.

Balance and pan properties were adjusted for the track in the session view and the waveform was exported again.

The display (right) now shows that the pan information is central. The waveform will now translate successfully to radio and TV.

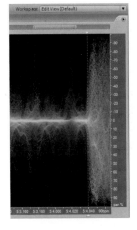

Frequency and phase windows

Additional tools are provided for real time analysis of frequency and phase. From the menu bar choose Window, Frequency analysis and Phase analysis. Both of these windows contain panels which can be dragged and docked into the current workspace.

The frequency analysis window (Alt+Z) (middle right) produces a real time moving frequency graph showing concentration of frequencies under the moving track cursor, Use each of the four hold buttons to grab line snapshots of the frequency curve at any time. Deselect the linear option to produce a natural logarithmic curve.

The phase window (Alt+X) (lower right) produces a dramatic visual representation of the phase information contained in the waveform. The window has two axis; the x-axis (horizontal) contains side information (left – right). The y-axis (vertical) plots mid information (left + right). The Chart Type menu at the bottom of the graph enables several display options from the default histogram to the Phase wheel plotting frequency amplitude and phase in position. When in the histogram mode, right click over the graph to show additional options for peaks and valleys. Right click and drag over the scale on each axis to zoom into the graph. The samples menu provides options for the number of samples to be displayed concurrently. Options up to around 16000 samples provide a dramatic moving graph indicating the current phase information under the moving cursor. Above 16000 samples the time required to process the information exceeds the time available to display the information and so the graph cannot move.

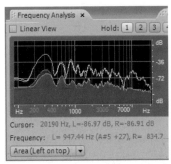

Copying and pasting within the edit view

Waveform data can be copied and pasted just like any other sort of data within a document. This ability enables damaged sections of a waveform to be repaired using similar sections from elsewhere. In the Spectral Frequency View small sections of the waveform can be selected by frequency and moved or copied elsewhere. This process is destructive as the edits are saved over the original waveform unless 'Save As' is used to create a new file.

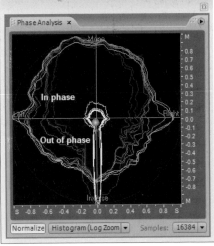

Data is copied to five temporary clipboards or the default Windows clipboard. Press Ctrl + 1 to Ctrl + 5 to select each clipboard (the current clipboard is shown in the status bar) or Ctrl + 6 to choose the Windows clipboard. The clipboard must be selected before the data is pasted to the clipboard. If a clipboard is not selected the data will be stored in the Windows Clipboard. Copied data is stored in the clipboard only until the program is closed. Copy sections of the waveform to the selected clipboard using the right click menu functions; Cut and Copy. Alternatively use the options in the File Menu on the Menu Bar.

1   Select any area of data by left clicking and dragging with the time selection tool. Use shortcut keys (H,J,K and L if set in keyboard shortcuts) to shrink or

expand the range. Alternatively zoom in on the area to be processed and place markers (F8) at the beginning and end points of the selected area. Left click and drag Markers with sample accuracy.

2   Right click and select copy or paste from the menu. Copying data leaves the selected area intact. Cutting data removes the selected area from the waveform. If no area is selected the entire waveform is copied.

Choose Edit>Select Entire Wave (or press Ctl+A) to copy the entire waveform to the clipboard. Remember to recall the correct clipboard before pasting.

Tip

Although it's possible to move frequencies in time, it's not possible to convert frequencies to other frequencies simply by moving the selected area in the view. The paste operation will paste the selected range of frequencies back into the same range at the point at which the start position marker (yellow line) is placed.

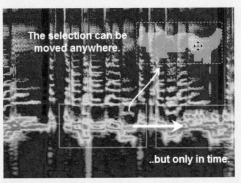

Paste (Ctl + V) inserts the contents of the clipboard at the current position of the playback cursor.

Paste to new (Ctl + Shift + N) loads the contents of the clipboard into the edit view as a new file.

Mix paste (Ctl + Shift + V) pastes the currently selected clipboard at the play-back cursor over any existing data. The clipboard data is merged with the exist-ing data according to selections made in the mix paste dialog. The volume slider values are shown as percentages so 100 will paste the new data over the exist-ing data at the same level as the original. Choosing 'Loop Paste' repeats the con-tents of the clipboard as many times as you wish. Contents may be pasted from the last used clipboard (close dialog and press Ctrl + 1 through 5 to select another clipboard), the Windows clipboard or from a file.

Tip

The option to select just the current view to the clipboard is not selected by default. Change this option in Edit, Preferences, General Tab. Choose the option for View in edit view Selections.

Insert	Inserts clipboard data at playback cursor
Overlap	Mixes contents of clipboard with existing data at levels set with slider
Replace	Replaces samples to length of contents of clipboard
Modulate	Waveform inherits amplitude of contents of clipboard
Crossfade	Fades the clipboard data in and out to the value specified here

Alternatively choose a file to paste at the selected point.

The effects menu

Adobe Audition 2.0 has forty seven effects available in the edit view. Effects are divided into six categories, each category containing both VST effects and Audition Process effects. Process effects cannot be used in real time but typically they offer a larger range of options than the real time effect. Both VST and process versions of some of the effects (Amplitude and Hard Limiting) are provided.

Effects are applied to the selected range or to the whole waveform if no range is selected. If part of the waveform is hidden, the effect can be applied to just the current view (the part of the waveform revealed between the left and right edges of the frame) or to the hidden parts of waveform. This option is set in Preferences (F4) in the General tab; edit view selections.

Edit undo

With the exception of the mastering rack every process in the edit view is destructive and in the case of the entire waveform is applied over the last process. Adobe Audition 2.0 provides a number of undo levels. By default the number is 5. This can be changed in the System tab of the Preferences dialogue (F4). Each undo level takes additional disk space but 10 or more levels can easily be used with no adverse side effects. If disk space becomes a problem purge the undo cache.

Changes to the waveform are not made until the waveform is finally saved. Waveforms with unsaved changes are identified with a * alongside the file name in the files panel.

VST and Direct X effects

Real time VST effects developed by third parties are used in the Adobe Audition 2.0 edit view and in the multitrack effects racks. VST processes can be unpredictable and under developed VST effects can cause Adobe Audition to exit abnormally 'crash'.

Add / Remove VST Directory

To install VST effects simply copy the .dll file supplied with the effect into any folder. Choose Effects, Add Remove VST folder to direct Adobe Audition to the VST files. Reload Adobe Audition after installing additional effects.

Effects developed to use the Microsoft Direct X layer are called Direct X effects. Direct X effects are installed with a program installer. Close Adobe Audition before installing new Direct X effects and refresh the effects list using the option in the effects menu to enable Adobe Audition to find and recognise the new effect. Direct X and VST effects are listed in the effects menu and enabled in mixer and mastering effects racks.

Using effects in the Mastering Rack

Typically effects in the edit view are applied serially (one at a time) and as such the effect of one effect on the next effect to be applied cannot be heard. When more than one effect is to be applied, the mastering rack is a convenient and powerful tool to use. The mastering rack is essentially an effects rack from the multitrack view, taken out of the mixer panel and imported into the edit view. Effects are placed in the mastering rack in the same way as in the Mixer Panel.

1 Left click on the small triangle to the right of the empty effects list.
2 Choose a VST effect from the lmenu
3 Adjust effects paramters to suit or choose from an effects preset
4 If necessary adjust wet/dry levels

Press the play button at the bottom of the effects rack to preview the various effects on the waveform. The green Power On/Off button is green when effects are applied and grey when the effects are muted.

Pre-roll and post-roll can be enabled when applying effects over a range. This option adds one second to the start and end section of the preview. Preroll and Postroll options are placed in the edit view under the Options

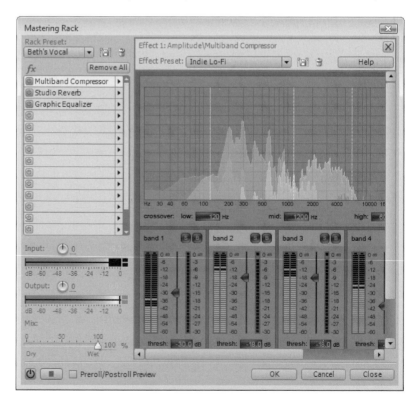

menu. The option to enable Preroll and Postroll is set for all effects that support this function in the menu; Effects,Enable Preroll and Postroll preview.

Creating a simple mastering tool with the mastering rack

Publishing or distributing audio without preparation is a little like framing a picture before the paint has dried. The painting may have looked fantastic to the artist in the studio. But outside, the paint will run or become damaged and the artwork will never be seen how the artist intended it.

Mastering is finishing and putting the audio inside a sonic 'frame'. In the early days of commercial music the finished tape recording had to be turned into a metal 'master' record with which vinyl records were stamped. This was and is managed by the mastering engineer; a highly skilled audio engineer who can take an analogue stereo recording and create a CD, DVD or even a vinyl LP which can be relied on to play accurately on a wide range of equipment in almost any environment. In the digital domain mastering is a similar task; taking stereo waveforms and applying highly selective compensation with the intention of making sure that the resulting Mp3, iTune, CD or soundtrack is the highest possible quality and will play equally well on any equipment or media.

There are as many disciplines, theories and opinions about mastering in the digital domain as there are people. Some guidelines are always agreed on, no matter who is leading the discussion;

1 When mixing down, never over apply compression. Dynamic range is what makes music exciting. Removing dynamic range in an attempt to maximise track loudness will ruin your track or song.
2 Always leave at least 3dB of headroom in the stereo master. Leave more if your track is to be sent away for commercial production.
3 Critically listen to your tracks in a number of environments. If your listening environment is not acoustically compensated, listen to your tracks in as many environments as possible.

The processes used to finally shape and smooth the audio are equally diverse. Two processes are nearly always used, no matter what the program or the destination;

1 EQ. Compensate and remove peaks in the stereo mix using high quality Parametric EQ.
2 Multiband Compression. Apply different levels of compression to each part of the frequency spectrum using the Multiband Compressor.

Adobe Audition 2.0 provides all the tools required for mastering your stereo waveform inside the program.

Mastering a session

1 Create a finished session in the multitrack view. Use automation, effects and track EQ to produce a high quality stereo mix. Always leave at least 6dB of headroom at the Master Track outputs and examine meters

(particularly buss track meters for evidence of clipping. Red segments will appear in level meters in tracks that are clipping. Tracks and buss tracks should peak at a maximum of -3dB. It's not necessary to produce finished audio in the session. In fact it's preferable to leave some rough edges – particularly at the beginning and end of the session. Noise before and at the end of the track is much easier to deal with in stereo. On the other hand – work as hard as possible to remove noise from individual tracks lying in the session. Noise quickly accumulates inside the track and is impossible to remove from the mixdown stereo wave.

2 From the File menu choose 'File, Export Audio Mixdown' Save the exported file in Windows PCM format and at the session bit rate.

3 Open the stereo waveform in the edit view and open the Mastering Rack (Effects, Mastering Rack)

Populate the mastering rack with three simple effects;

• Parametric EQ
• Stereo expander
• Multiband compressor

Parametric EQ

Parametric EQ is used to flatten peaks or curves that may be difficult for equipment to reproduce. At the same time it can add shape to a track that needs something to bring it out of the ordinary. At all times the role of EQ at this stage is not to be heard. Use very small amounts of cut or boost over the entire spectrum.

• Second order shelf at 34Hz, Very few systems are able to reproduce frequencies below this. Apply a shelf in this area to remove muddiness from the mix and tighten the bass frequencies.

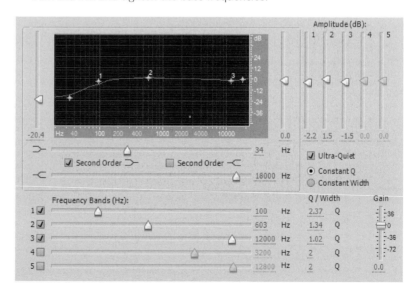

- -2.2 cut at 100Hz. Dependent on your program. Can produce clarity in the low mids particularly on rock bass guitar.
- 1.5 boost at 603Hz. Adds presence in the critical mid frequencies. Experiment with Q to avoid smearing the upper mids.
- -1.5dB cut at 12kHz. Just removing a tiny amount in the upper frequencies adds 'air' to productions with strong vocal content.

Stereo expander

The stereo expander effect widens the stereo field and allows detail to come through, particularly in busy mixes. However, the effect will also remove bass frequencies.

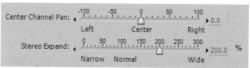

Adobe Audition 2.0 includes the Izotope Multiband Compression VST effect (right). This is a powerful tool which can add punch and presence to rock music. The compressor divides the frequency spectrum into four bands;

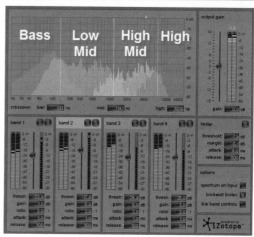

Band 1	Bass	Blue
Band 2	Low-Mid	Orange
Band 3	High-Mid	Green
Band 4	High	Pink

Multiband compressor

Dynamics for each band can be adjusted without affecting other bands. For instance; excessive sibilance in a vocal can be compensated for in the high mid section. Sibilance is impossible to remove using parametric EQ because the range of frequencies is very narrow and the amount of sibilance is continually changing. The multiband compressor allows for a limit to be set using the threshold control. Below the threshold the sibilant frequencies are not affected. Above the threshold the sibilance is reduced by the amount in the gain control. Drag and move the white separator rulers to change the crossover point between each frequency range. Use the S and B buttons in each band to solo or bypass (mute) that range.

Select and apply dynamics to each band of frequencies. Then, use the link band control at the far right to group each band and apply an overall level of threshold. The limiter section enables overall limiting for the entire frequency spectrum.

The multiband compressor is provided with several presets which are a great place to start experimenting. Don't be heavy handed though. The Broadcast preset in particular is a textbook example of how a track can be maximised by removing almost all the dynamics from the program. On the other hand using the Broadcast preset on a radio advert will almost certainly grab the listeners' attention and will definitely carry your message across.

As with track effects racks, individual effect settings can be saved and the entire rack settings can also be saved as a preset. If the settings for the entire rack are saved as a preset it is not necessary to save individual effect settings.

Effects rack in the edit view

If 'Remove All' is used to remove all effects you will see a warning message declaring that automation will also be deleted along with the effects. There is no automation in the edit view and this message can be safely ignored.

Process tools in the effects menu

Along with Effects, a few simple editing tools have been placed in the effects menu above the VST and Process effects.

Invert (process)

Converts positive values into their negative equivalents or vice versa. Use invert when resolving phase problems in the time domain.

Reverse (process)

Reverse (play backwards) the range or the whole waveform if no range is selected.

Mute (silence)

Replaces every sample in the range (or in the whole waveform if no range is selected) with a zero value. In this way the waveform is muted but the number of samples within the waveform is not changed therefore the length of the waveform is unchanged.

Tip

If you have an acoustic guitar piece with many pauses you may consider that silence in the pauses would be a good idea, especially if there is audience noise etc. However pure silence is unnatural (even in space). Instead, copy a few seconds from the beginning or end of the concert and mix paste in the pauses. The mix paste feature enables data from any of the five clipboards, a file or the Windows Clipboard to be pasted into or over existing data. The data can be repeated (Loop Paste) and crossfaded in which case the current data will fade out while the pasted data is faded in according to values in the Mix Paste dialog. Inserting the data simply moves the existing data to the right and fills the gap with the contents of the clipboard. Overlap places the new data on top of the current data with amplitude decided by the Volume fader. Replace deletes as much existing data as is necessary to accommodate the clipboard data. Modulate modulates the current data with the existing data.

Process effects and VST effects

Choose and apply process and VST effects from this menu. Effects are applied to the selected range or the entire waveform.

Amplitude effects

Use amplitude effects when the waveform requires cutting or boosting in volume. Stereo expansion is a psycho-acoustic effect created by manipulating amplitude values, which is why it appears in this section.

Amplify (boost or cut volume, apply gliding fades)
Amplify / fade (process)
Binaural auto-panner (process, stereo only)
Channel mixer (stereo only)
Dynamics processing (compression/expansion)
Envelope process(apply fade in/fade out)
Hard limiting (mastering tool)
Hard limiting (process) normalise (set maximum amplitude of waveform)
Multiband compressor
Normalise (process)
Pan expand (process)(stereo only)
Stereo expander
Stereo field rotate (stereo only)
Stereo field rotate (process)

Delay effects

Delay effects include echo, delay and reverbs. Some delay effects such as complex reverbs are unsuitable for use in the multitrack view.

Chorus
Delay
Dynamic delay (process)(apply delay over time)
Echo
Echo chamber (complex echo)
Flanger
Full Reverb (complex reverb)
Multitap delay
Reverb
Studio reverb
Sweeping phaser

Filters

Adobe Audition 2.0 includes EQ processes in the filters group. Sweeping resonance and synth filters are not included. For general EQ use the Graphic Equaliser or the Parametric Equaliser. The Graphic Phase shifter is not the traditional 'Phaser' effect, Use the Sweeping Phaser in the delay section instead.

Centre channel expander
Dynamic EQ (process)(apply EQ over time)
FFT filter (process)(very precise EQ)
Graphic equaliser
Graphic phase shifter
Notch filter (surgically remove specific frequencies)
Parametric equaliser (most useful EQ)
Quick filter (process)
Scientific filters (process)

Noise reduction

Noise Reduction, Click Eliminators etc. are restoration effects. Restoration is the process of cleaning sound away from the program or required audio in order to make the audio meaningful. At one end of the scale this is simple click removal from a dithered track. On the other hand the noise restoration tools are regularly used to clean telephone and scientific recordings etc.

Auto click pop eliminator (process)(find and remove clicks and pops from noisy recording)
Click pop eliminator (process)
Clip restoration (process)(smooths badly clipped recording)
Hiss reduction (process)(de-essing)
Noise reduction (process)(analyse and remove noise)

Special

Special effects are used when the character of the waveform needs to be changed.

Convolution (process)(waveform takes on character of another from stored impulse)
Distortion (odd distortion tool)

Time pitch

Time pitch effects are unusual time based effects such as the Pitch Bender and Pitch Shifter. Also included are restorative processes such as the Pitch Correction (Auto-Tune) tool.

Doppler shifter (process)(very realistic movement simulation)
Pitch bender (process)(great for special fx)
Pitch correction (process)
Pitch shifter recycle waveform to change pitch or tempo)
Stretch (process)

Amplitude and envelope effects

Amplitude, amplify

The VST Amplify effect is used to add or remove power from the waveform.

Amplitude, amplify/fade (process)

Amplify / Fade is a process effect for adjusting amplitude power. Levels are expressed by either percentage or in dB depending on the presence of a check mark in the dialog. Move the slider to the left to decrease level or to the right to increase level. Values can also be entered manually. If the mouse is clicked over the slider, values can be incremented using the left and right cursor keys. DC Bias Adjust will compensate for a poorly performing sound card by placing the centre of the waveform on the centre line. Choose the 'Differential' option to automatically do this or enter a value manually if you

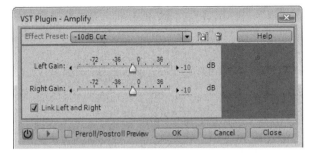

want to shift the waveform off centre. Clicking the Fade tab produces two faders. The upper fader is the level of the waveform 'pre-fade' the lower waveform is the level of the 'post fade' wave. Choosing two different values will produce a smooth linear fade over the selected area. Use the Logarithmic option to produce a stronger fade effect. Preview the effect before applying.

Amplitude, binaural auto panner (process)

In Cool Edit this was the Brainwave Synchroniser. Essentially a highly scientific and effective auto-panning tool. Create panning movement along the waveform by dragging handles within the graph to top or bottom. Works on stereo waverforms only.

Amplitude, channel mixer

Stereo Waveforms only. The Channel Mixer combines information from both sides of a stereo waveform to create stereo effects such as vocal cut or stereo imaging. Top of the tree for useful things in the list of presets is the Vocal Remover. By inverting the Left and Right channels the information in the centre channel is lost through phase cancellation leaving only the information panned hard left and right at mixdown. Unfortunately this means losing drums and some other parts depending on the recording but the creative possibilities are very exciting.

Amplitude, dynamics processing

Process Compression and Expansion tool

Compression is used to lower dynamic range in a waveform by reducing the difference between quiet and loud sounds. Levels below the threshold are amplified and very high levels are reduced. This enables the overall level of the waveform to be increased without clipping and makes quiet sounds more apparent in the mix.

Expansion is the opposite to compression. Sounds below the input threshold are attenuated in order to remove background noise for instance. Sounds above the threshold are boosted.

A *limiter* imposes a ceiling at which all sounds are instantly attenuated. Such limiters are often called 'brick wall' compressors as the amplitudes are simply chopped back to the threshold limit rather than being gently attenuated depending on the input level.

Noise gating is a simple type of expansion. Levels below the input threshold are very heavily attenuated. The result is the creation almost of a switch, cutting the sound off when it reaches a certain level. Noise gating can be used as a very simple form of noise reduction (although for much better results use the comprehensive noise reduction effects) but post digital-domain is now much more often used as a retro special effect.

Create those cool 1980's 'big drum' sounds using noise gating:

- Load a suitably retro acoustic tom or kick drum sample
- Apply some serious reverb – well over the top
- Apply dynamics processing. Use the Noise Gate at 10dB and feel it *In the air tonight!*

Overview

The main feature of the Dynamics Processing dialog box is a large graph with input (X, left to right) and output values (Y, up and down) calibrated in dB. The centre line shows a waveform that is untouched as each value in the input axis has the same value on the output axis. Click the mouse over the centre line in the graph to add 'nodes' to the line and drag nodes to the edge of the box to delete. For example, choose the 2:1, -20 Fast Drums preset from the list of presets in the dialog. The graph shows that any information under –20dB will be attenuated gradually by a ration of 2:1 until data with an amplitude of 0db arriving at the input of the compressor at 0db is attenuat-

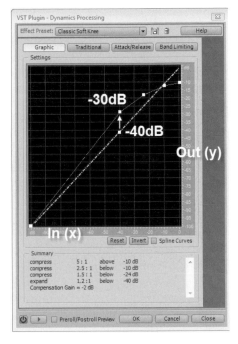

ed to –10db. To compensate for this the output gain is boosted by 6db.

Use the mouse to click on the line at the point where the input and output values meet at -30db. Drag the new handle left along the green line by two 'squares' until it reaches the –50dB threshold on the input (x) axis. This new line enables expansion to be applied below a threshold of –50dB and compression to be applied below a threshold of –20db. Parts of the waveform arriving at the input of Dynamics Processing with amplitude of –50dB would be boosted by 20dB to –30dB. Below –50dB amplitudes are gradually attenuated to increase the signal to noise ratio. This means that quiet passages of music between –20db and –30db will be amplified slightly according to the input level while amplitudes under –50dB will quietly be attenuated.

This curve will amplify very quiet sounds in the waveform, leaving louder sounds unchanged. On speech this would aid clarity but increase background noise. Over an orchestra recorded in a quiet room this curve would enhance tiny sounds (such as a whispering audience or a soft passage) giving the impression of more detail or even a better recording. To manually enter threshold and ratio values use the 'traditional' tab or right click on any node within the graphics page to see the details for that section. Use the 'splines' option to produce subtle 'soft knee' compression effects that are very suitable for vocals. The Dynamics Processor includes powerful tools for Gain Processing and Level Detection, etc. but does not include any sidechain. Sidechaining in Adobe Audition (using the amplitude of one instrument to control the amplitude of another) is performed using a multitrack transform called 'Envelope Follower' and is discussed elsewhere in this book.

Band limiting

A side effect of compression is to attenuate the high frequencies in the mix. This can be avoided by limiting the compression effect to a band of frequencies only. This is known as band limiting. The Adobe Audition 2.0 multiband compressor VST effect provides four bands of compression across the entire spectrum. The dynamic processor VST effect enables band limiting in a slightly different way by providing an upper and lower limit. Compression is not applied to frequencies above and below these parameters. Band limiting has a number of applications from reducing noise in a waveform to increasing the apparent level of a bass guitar without overly affecting the level of the vocal.

For example; you have a stereo drum track recorded using two or three good quality microphones but somehow the snare and kick need emphasis.

1 Load the stereo waveform and drag a range to select a small section of the drummer in full flow. (previewing a four minute wave takes a long time so try the transform on a selection first).
2 In the Dynamics Processor choose the Full Reset preset and preview the effect over the drums. You will hear no change as the input and output levels are completely level.
3 From the preset list choose the Fat Snare preset.
4 Click over the Band Limiting button and enter 200 in the low cutoff and 600 in the high cutoff. Compression is now only applied to the midrange frequencies, including the snare which should now be more apparent.

With a little care you can tune the frequency range to the shape and frequency of the snare drum. Kick drums occupy 75Hz – 150Hz. Use this technique to make the low frequencies punchier although it's a careful balancing act between this and the snare.

This technique is also very useful for enlivening old LP's and tapes before burning to CD. A dull bass part could also be brought to life by identifying the frequencies of the accent notes and emphasising those frequencies accordingly.

The Dynamic Processor effect is a destructive effect and care should be used when processing as the compression effect is sometimes more apparent after a period of rest, overnight for instance. This is because the ear has a natural ability to compress sound (we do this naturally at night as our hearing alerts us to 'things that go bump'). Use File, Save Copy As to save a copy of the file while working on the original just in case.

Amplitude, Envelope (Process)

The Envelope effect is used to create amplitude curves over the waveform. Applications for envelopes include the famous fade in and fade out curve. Envelopes can also be used for removing 'plosives' (hard 'p' sounds created at the front of such words as 'pop' and 'put'). Use the Fade In preset to remove the front part of the wave and back the effect off until the plosive isn't a problem.

Envelopes in the edit view are used to shape the waveform itself. The envelope effect allows the drawing of a envelope curve over the selected area or the entire waveform if no area is selected. Click the mouse over the centre line to produce a 'node' that is then pushed into place. To remove a node drag it to the right or left until it either meets another node or the side of the box. To add level to the envelope increase the 'Amplification' value past %100. Checking 'Spline Curves' produces a smooth envelope. This is a very creative effect that can produce dramatic effects.

When creating long fades with the envelopes tool, try to mimic the way that the engineer or producer would use the master fader. Natural fades seem to start almost imperceptibly but tail off steeply towards the end of the fade. A concave bow in the graph produces a fade that will keep the attention of the listener right to the end.

Amplitude, Hard Limiting

Hard Limiting attenuates sound exceeding a preset threshold. This produces an effect similar to that of the broadcast limiter. Hard limiting produces a non musical effect best used on radio speech. The VST Hard Limiting effect can be automated using automation lanes in the multitrack view.

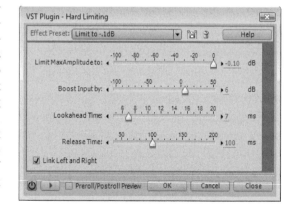

Amplitiude, Hard Limiting (Process)

The Hard Limiting Process effect is an amplitude levelling tool for waveforms with a consistent level except for occasional large 'spikes' maybe caused by cymbal crash or other transient sounds. Hard Limiting reduces and softens the level of the 'spikes' while amplifying the rest of the waveform accordingly. If used without care this will totally destroy the dynamics of a musical piece. However it's useful in small doses for mastering live recordings or spoken word.

Hard limiting is very useful for reducing the dynamic range of final mixes, especially Top 40 material intended for radio play or for creating radio advertisements that really spring out at the audience. Use the values in the Hard Limiter dialog to tune the effect to suit your material. The Statistics function shows what percentage of the waveform would clip if hard limiting were not applied. When working with 16bit samples set the Limit Max Amplitude control to -.5 dB to enable maximum headroom. The Hard Limiting process effect is destructive and has no automation. Make a copy of the file before applying the effect over a critical waveform.

Amplitude, multiband compressor

Use the multiband compressor as a mixdown tool or as an insert in an effects rack. The multiband compressor can be used on stereo or mono waveforms.

The compressor has four independent frequency bands with adjustable crossovers. An overall limiting function enables global control over the output of the effect. Solo each band in turn and adjust the crossover by dragging the white rulers along the frequency spectrum until the band is wide or narrow enough to accommodate the target frequency band. Lower the threshold level until the meters indicate that the threshold is reached as the waveform peaks. Adjust attack, release and gain controls. Repeat for the other three frequency bands then use the global limiting control to avoid clipping.

The multiband compressor is a VST effect with automation when used in the multitrack mixer panel. Any of the Multiband controls can be automated.

Tip

Use automation to apply a little more compression to the chorus sections of your song and compensate by raising the level of the chorus in the track. Back off the threshold during the verse sections to create contrast in the song.

Normalize (Process)

Use the Normalising effect when you need to raise the overall level of the waveform. Normalising calculates the difference between the loudest peak in the range or waveform and maximum amplitude (0dBfs). This number is then added to each sample. The effect of this is to increase the overall amplitude in relation to the loudest peak. The amount by which the entire waveform (or section) is amplified depends on the maximum values within the waveform. So a waveform with a single peak of −3dB would receive an overall boost of 3dB (if normalising was set to %100). A waveform with a large dynamic range, such as a percussion solo, will not benefit much from normalising. For instance a snare roll peaking at −2dB will only produce a 2dB boost – not much good if your soft triangle part is at −20dB. Use the Normalise effect 'pre-production' to boost a low amplitude waveform bearing in mind that any noise will also be normalised at the same time. For details of how to use normalise as a mastering aid see 'RMS Normalising of CD compilation in preparation for burning'.

Tip

Waveforms used in a session need to be normalised. Normalising will enable clips to be balanced more easily and will require less automation. In the files panel click or shift select the session waveforms. Right click and choose 'Group Waveform Normalize' from the menu.

Pan and Expand (Process)

Expands the stereo panorama by recalculating levels inside the waveform. Use the VST stereo expansion effect if this is required during mastering or in real time.

If the Pan / Expand transform is applied to a musical piece, the effect is very mild. However on a spoken word soundtrack or radio production the effect is more pronounced and produces realistic '3D' imaging from a conventional stereo waveform. The clearest way to examine this effect is to generate a stereo wave-form containing a few seconds of white noise generated using the 'Spatial Stereo' option. This option produces two channels of white noise delayed by whatever value is appropriate, usually around 500ms. Apply the pan expand effect over the white noise to hear Adobe Audition split the noise into low and high fre-quency bands then pan the bands to alternate sides of the stereo image.

Stereo Expander

Widens the stereo field in realtime and can be use in mastering racks and effect racks. Use as a mastering tool to enhance detail in a busy mix and as an effect by vary-ing the amount of the expansion at different points in the audio. Can be automated using the automation lanes.

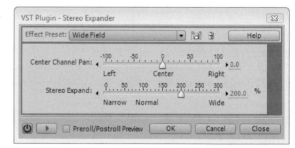

Stereo Field Rotate

Use the stereo field rotate effect to rebalance waveforms which are pro-nounced on either side of the stereo field. Can be used in real time as a VST effect and can be automated. The Stereo Field Rotate effect is a mastering tool and can be used in the mastering rack.

Stereo Field Rotate (Process)

Produces moving pan effects when applied to a stereo waveform. The effects are subtle but great for adding the illusion of movement to a soundtrack, two people having a conversation while walking down a hallway for instance. Creating movement is very simple. The graph plots time against degrees. To create a simple pan for instance all that is necessary is to draw a line that bisects the graph top left to bottom right. If necessary a more complex graph can be created and made to loop over the selected range.

Delay Effects

Native delay effects include the usual Reverb and Delays etc. as well as some 'special' effects such as the impressive Sweeping Phaser and Dynamic Echo.

Chorus

Chorus is a VST chorus effect produced by creating layers of the input and applying different levels of delay and modulation to each layer. The result is a rich lush sound, especially suited to guitars and backing vocals. The chorus effect also has the effect of widening the stereo image slightly. This effect will remove some of the bass frequencies in the audio. The effect can be automated and is light on the processor.

For guitar players the Adobe Audition effect includes all the features found in hardware effects. The use of the chorus effect is fairly straightforward and the developers have obviously had some fun creating the presets. Listen to a few of the presets and apply over backing vocals, strings guitars etc. In the effects rack insert a compressor before the chorus and delay after to produce a lush swirling guitar sound. Binaural cues are best when your mix is to be played on headphones as the effect can sound off balance through speakers.

Delay

Stereo delay with independent delay and level controls for each channel. If used on a mono source the mono signal is divided and sent to each channel. This VST effect is fully automated and perfectly suited for creative mixing. Delay introduces small amounts of delay into each or both of the stereo channels up to a maximum of 500ms. The presets explore this effect very thoroughly with effects from slapback tape echo to Elvis impressions! The vocal presence presets can produce great results on poorly recorded vocals.

Dynamic Delay (Process)

The dynamic delay effect enables delay effects to be drawn over a graph inside the effect window. In this way the delay effect can change over the length of a waveform or over the length of a range.

The dialog box contains two graphs. The upper graph dictates the amount of time (up to 50ms) by which the dry signal will be delayed. The lower graph dictates the amount of feedback that will be introduced to the delayed sound. The Y axis of the graph indicates time. This axis shows either the entire waveform or just the selection, depending on your decision. For this example I've used 10 seconds of white noise in order to clearly hear the effect. Click on the line in the upper graph to create a new node. Drag this new node to the upper edge of the graph at about 1 sec. Note the status field just under the graph indicates the values under the cursor.

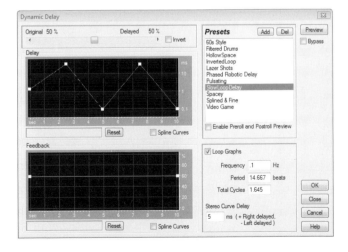

Create another node at 5 secs and -1ms, and finally a third at 7secs and 50ms. The centre line is at 1ms. Press the preview button to hear the flanging effect.

In the lower graph create one node with a value of 80% at 2 seconds. Press preview again to hear the flanging effect again. Notice how the effect is more pronounced over the first five seconds as the feedback intensifies this portion of the wave. This deliberately simple example uses a regular frequency but of course the real value of this effect is the ability to produce effects which can be tailored to suit the waveform. Imagine a heavy metal guitar solo in which the performer is using the tremolo arm with irregular frequency. Wouldn't it be great to apply the flanging effect exactly in time with each movement of the arm?

An irregular waveform can be made to loop in regular intervals by checking the Loop Graphs checkbox. Notice the Y axis changes to represent the value in the Period field. The flanging effect will now loop at this frequency over the waveform. Changing the values in any one of the Loop Graph fields will cause the program to calculate new values for the other fields.

Echo

Delay effects delay a part of the input signal on its way to the output. Echo takes part of the input signal and repeats it over and over again to produce a repeated sound. The EQ of repeats can also be changed as the echo effect dies away. These properties enable complex and musical echo effects to be produced, such as the effect of a wrench dropped into a lift shaft for instance. The echo effect has two inputs, each input has separate controls for Delay Time, Feedback and Echo Level. Adjust the Delay Time control to change the speed of the repeated sound and adjust the feedback to control the amount of echo signal sent back into the input. This effect is a VST effect with full automation possibilities.

Analogue and digital echo devices have been around for as long as tape recorders. The Adobe Audition Echo effect introduces the ability to attenuate frequencies within the echo repeats to produce interesting 'lo-fi' echo effects. As with each of the effects the presets are the best place to start experimenting.

Echo Chamber

The Echo Chamber effect is more complex than the plain Echo effect as it enables the specification of room sizes and characteristics in order to simulate (as far as the effect is able to) actual listening environments. The difficulty with this effect is that the interface requires numeric values to be calculated or measured for the required environment but it is remarkably effective. This effect is particularly good for spoken word (or dialogue). The effect is too complex for a musical piece although spectacular special effects can be produced with this effect. This effect requires more processing than simpler effects and preview isn't immediate, be patient if previewing large range selections. See the help file for detailed descriptions of each parameter.

Flanger

The Flanger is a VST effect which recreates the classic 'Jet Plane' effect typical of nearly any record from the late sixties and early seventies. The effect is produced by delaying and phase shifting a variable portion of the input and recombining this with the output. Flanging is very effective when used on pads and slow sounds such as low orchestral pads. Flanging also occurs naturally in nature and is an effective tool when recreating natural sounds.

Edit the values in the Flanger effect dialog box to produce a dramatic 'Jet Plane' effect:

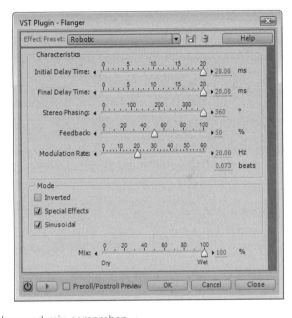

Full Reverb

The Full Reverb effect is the most complex reverb and the most natural sounding. Full Reverb uses convolution impulses to create the effect and so avoids the introduction of artefacts such as metallic or ringing sounds. This effect is CPU intensive and will slow the rendering of a background mix comprehensively therefore it is recommended that the Full Reverb effect is used mainly within the edit view. Use the sliders or enter values in the dialog box to create reverb sounds.

Reverberation

Decay Time	Reverb decay
Pre-Delay Time	Pre delay or envelope. Essentially how long the reverb will take to reach full effect
Diffusion	High diffusion for smooth reverb or low diffusion for more echo in the reflections
Perception	Builds variations in the effect so as to sound more natural

Early Reflections

Room Size	The volume of the room in cubic meters
Dimension	The ratio between the width and depth of the room
Left-Right Location	Simulates the effect of the source being placed to the right or left of the virtual room rather than dead centre
High Pass Cutoff	Prevents low frequency loss in small room sizes. Use values between 80Hz and 150Hz
Set Reverb based on Room Size	If this option is selected the reverb properties will be calculated according to the room size.

The Colouration button produces a familiar EQ graph with frequency over the X axis and amplitude on the Y axis. Select frequency and amplitude by dragging handles around the graph or use the faders on the right and below. Set decay effects for the upper frequencies using the decay control on the right of the fader.

Colouration

Frequency (X)	Sweepable three band selection
Amplitude (Y)	Cut or boost of each frequency band.

Mixing Section

Dry	Amount of dry signal present in the mix
Wet	The amount of wet (reverb) signal in the mix
Early Reflections	Set at about half of the value of the original signal slider for natural reverb
Include Direct	Enhances the result when used with a stereo file over headphones to give a true stereo effect.
Sum left and right outputs	Combines the input signal to enable faster processing for when mono input source is pre sent.

Tip

Dry / Wet balance. If both dry and wet balance are set to 100% the output will be twice the input. When balancing dry and wet signals check that the sum of both doesn't exceed 100%. For instance a dry setting of 60% and a wet setting of 40% will produce a sum output of 100%

The Full Reverb effect is a VST effect and can be used in realtime with automation. However this effect is very heavy on the processor and is (probably) unsuitable for use in a multitrack session. However, YMMV.

Multitap Delay

Delay, echo, filter and reverb are combined inside this effect to produce complex and unusual effects. Up to ten echo devices can be chained in series to create extreme echo effects using this effect. As well as being chained together the devices can be placed inside each other. Each device has independent settings;

Delay Offset	Image is taken from the furthest point and mixed back to an earlier point
Delay Time	The time in milliseconds between the image and the delayed audio mixed back into the effect
Feedback	The amount of delayed signal to be fed back into the mix. Higher values create extreme amounts of noise.

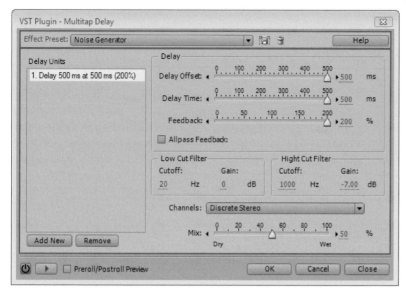

Pressing 'Add New' in the dialog creates another delay device. The current delay device is indicated by a red line in the delay plot while other devices have blue lines.

Allpass feedback	Enable to reduce clipping
Low and High Cut Filters	Enables filters to be created for each device independently so creating unusual effects such as all bass or all treble delay
Cutoff	The frequency at which the low or hi cut filter will affect the delay
Boost	A negative setting (-1) to attenuate frequencies above or below the threshold
Channels	Contains options for applying the effect to a stereo waveform.

Reverb

A simple reverb, very easy on the CPU. Use the simple reverb effect when using the reverb effect in effects racks as many effects can be applied to a session with no impact on performance. In Adobe Audition 1.5 this effect was called the Quickverb.

Studio Reverb

Studio Reverb presents reverb types and presets that are specifically tuned to the multitrack view or for use in the mastering rack. This is a convolution based VST effect which can be fully automated in the automation lanes but which requires fewer resources from the processor. The mastering reverb preset is great for smoothing of lead vocals.

Sweeping Phaser

The sweeping phaser effect is created by modulating a notch filter with a very narrow Q. This is a VST effect, often used on guitars but essential for manipulating noise when creating original sounds.

Sweep Gain	Boosts the effected sound coming back into the mix. Take care to avoid clipping
Centre Frequency	Set to the middle of the slider for best results or to the left and right for bass and treble phasing
Modulation Depth	The depth of the effect in Q (ratio of width to frequency)
Resonance	The amount of phase shift applied to the delayed portion of the signal
Modulation Rate	Speed of the effect. Useful as it enables the effect to be set to BPM (although not in sync with the session). Use fractions to set note values; a setting of 240 would produce quavers if the session tempo were 120bpm
Sweep Modes	Sinusoidal is the most common or triangular for special effects
Filter Type	If low pass option is chosen the effect will not be applied to any frequency below the threshold set by the centre frequency slider. Use logarithmic modulation for a deeper effect.
Master Gain	Instead of attempting to balance each of the values to produce a strong effect without clipping the Master Gain value enables the output to be attenuated

Filters and EQ

Filters are incredibly powerful tools for adjusting tone and volume. There is no limit to the way that these tools can be used imaginatively. Use the Parametric Equalizer for simple or complex frequency enhancement. Complex troubleshooting can also be performed using this tool. For example; You have recorded an acoustic guitar but the performer occasionally introduces 'string noise' into the recording. As the string noise is at a constant frequency it is possible to isolate it and soften it using parametric equalization. Select part of the waveform containing the string noise. Choose the preset called 'Reset To Zero' to flatten the curve and clear the bench. Press preview to hear the range selected earlier. The range will repeat until 'Stop' is selected. Put a checkmark in the centre frequency box 1 and push fader one on the right of the screen until a bell curve appears in the graph. Now move the centre frequency slider from right to left until the string noise becomes much more apparent. You are looking for the range of frequencies that match closely the frequencies in the string noise, probably centring on 6hkz. Depending on the string noise and the quality of the recording it's possible to narrow the width of the centre frequency to pinpoint almost exactly the frequency to be removed, Experiment with values of 80 to 100. When the string noise has been identified and boosted dramatically pull fader one down to a negative value (probably between –6 and –10dB) to soften the noise of the string without affecting the natural sound of the guitar. When it's right – press Stop to stop the playback and OK to apply the effect. It's important to perform this operation over just the areas affected by the string noise. Applying this procedure to the entire acoustic guitar track would remove 'good' sound that simply happened to coincide in the same frequency band. And of course you can save this setting as a Preset. Press the 'Add' button, enter a name for the preset (you can call it anything you like up to a limit of 62 characters eg: '6kHz String Noise remover') and store it for the next opportunity. After a while you'll own a library of instant presets for every job bringing editing time right down and your reputation as a pro, right up. Try doing that with four feet of racked equipment.

Precise editing and shaping of frequencies can be an incredibly creative tool. For instance a very boring drum sample can immediately be livened up simply by accenting one or more kicks or clicks within the sample. The classic 'telephone voice' vocal sound is a simple but highly effective effect (but go easy on it – it's often over used!) for picking out words or phrases within a vocal. Boosting frequencies with High 'Q' values (over 80) produces 'ringing tones', great for robotic vocals and special effects. At the other end of the scale, consistent mains hum (called 60 cycle hum) or noise produced by malfunctioning equipment can be very precisely 'notched out'. Adobe Audition has terrific, leading edge noise reduction tools but the Parametric equaliser is perfect for day to day bench work on difficult waveforms.

Aside from the parametric equaliser, the second most easily recognisable filter is the Graphic Equaliser. The graphic equaliser allows the creation of EQ 'Curves' which are applied to track length waveforms rather than small ranges or sections. Curves are useful as they enable the engineer to visually choose the desired shape of the frequency curve. However it's a blunt tool compared to the parametric equaliser and is often used for simple bass or treble lifts, etc. For example, you may have a bass guitar track which was recorded badly, leaving nothing in the middle frequencies. Because it was recorded badly there's little mileage in trying to identify the exact frequencies that need boosting. Instead, the engineer may try to simply apply a general curve to the whole bass track in an attempt to 'tune' it to the song and the other instruments. Adobe Audition enables you to add any filter to an effects rack and 'tune' the sound in real time while listening to the other instruments in the multitrack session. The graphic EQ offers 1 Octave (10 bands), ? Octave (20 Band) and 1/3 Octave (30 band) equalisers.

Centre Channel Extractor

The Centre Channel Extractor uses phase cancellation and modulation to produce the effect of a very wide centre channel by cancelling parts of the signal that occupy the centre area only. In effect this creates a 'hole' in the middle of the stereo field. The Centre Channel Extractor can be used as a creative effect – most often for extracting vocals from a commercial recording

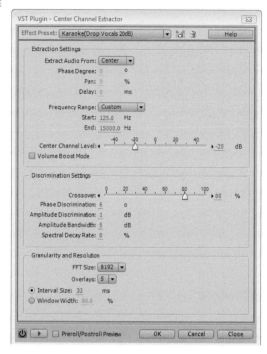

for instance. But the Centre Channel Extractor can also be used in scientific ways. One application for this effect is to widen the centre field in a 5.1 or 7.1 recording when preparing music for surround sound encoding.

Dynamic EQ (Process)

Dynamic EQ enables the gradual cut or boost of any frequency range over time. This effect can be used to produce 'bass kill' or 'treble kill' effects in dance music, Wah-Wah effects for guitars and many other creative effects.

Creating effects using Dynamic EQ

1 Create a waveform containing white noise of 10 seconds duration with an intensity of 12.
2 Invoke the Dynamic EQ dialog (Effects>Filters>Dynamic EQ). The dialog contains three graphs, similar in use to the Dynamic Delay effect. The uppermost graph dictates how much gain is applied over time. To hear this effect work it's necessary to create a graph which will cut 20dB of gain over the last five seconds of the waveform.
3 Reset each of the three graphs by clicking on the tab and reset button under the graph.
4 Return to the frequency graph and use the mouse pointer to create a new node by clicking on the blue line in the upper graph.
5 Create a node at 5 seconds and then drag the right handle as far as it can go to the bottom of the graph.
6 Switch to the gain tab. Create a new node at 5 seconds and drag the right handle as far as possible to the top of the graph. The third graph indicates 'Q'; a ratio of width to constant frequency.

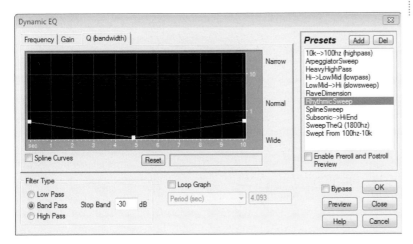

7 Create a new node at 5 seconds and drag the left handle as far as possible down to the bottom of the graph.

8 Press Preview to hear the filter effect as the high frequencies are gradually cut from the waveform until only the frequencies below 1000Hz (the centre line in the Frequency Graph remain.

The effect is very similar to surf on a beach. Use the high, low and band pass controls to hear different effects.

Creating a Wah-Wah effect

1 Load any suitably rhythmic guitar waveform or record a new part.

2 In the frequency tab move the centre line down to around 150 Hz at both ends.

3 Create another handle halfway along the line and drag up to around 22050Hz.

4 Ensure Spline Curves is enabled.

5 In the gain tab create another handle half way along the centre line and drag fractionally up to create a boost of about 8db. Again ensure spliine curves is enabled.

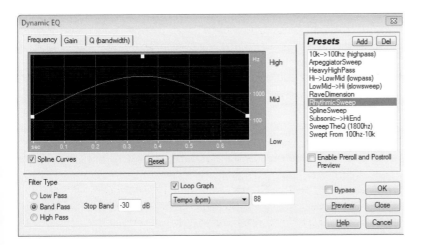

6   Enable the Loop Graph feature and choose BPM from the drop down box then enter the session tempo.

7   Choose Band Pass in the Filter Type options.

FFT Filter (Process)

This EQ filter uses a Fast Fourier Transform algorithm. FFT algorithms determine power versus frequency. They are scientific algorithms and when used over audio frequencies produce very scientific results. In particular the FFT is adept at scientific tasks over which involve precise calculations over just a small part of the frequency band. Use the FFT Filter when presented with an EQ task that involves 'notching out' very small frequency bands, for example when removing air conditioning noise from a recording. FFT filters are also useful when creating Band Pass filter (which reject frequencies above and below pre-set thresholds), Low Pass or High Pass filters. If you have access to specifications from mixing desk manufacturers or manufacturers of outboard equipment it is possible to build tools to mimic the effect of recording equipment hardware on a waveform.

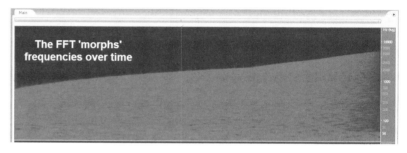

Changes to the frequency band can be applied over time if the Lock To Constant Filter option is deselected. When used in this way the selected options are gradually applied over the length of the range or the waveform. The FFT Filter also allows the waveform to be 'morphed' from one state to another. If the morphing option is not selected the FFT effect will filter just the bands selected in the graph. If the morphing option is checked the filter will transition through the frequency range, effectively changing the character of the whole waveform instead of just the selected frequencies. Enable morphing by removing the default checkmark from the 'Lock To Constant Filter' setting. To create target curves or notches choose the 'View Final' option in the top right hand corner of this dialog. Be aware that the preview function does not work when morphing is enabled in this effect. See the comprehensive Adobe Audition Help for detailed instructions regarding this filter. The notch filter (also available from the Filter menu) offers a very precise method of producing the same results by requiring numeric values from the user rather than presenting a graphical interface. In this way it is possible to surgically remove up to six fixed frequencies without affecting any other frequency above or below.

Graphic Equalizer

Graphic Equalizers have faders at preset frequency intervals. Selected frequencies are managed simply by cutting or boosting using the fader. Graphic

EQ is easy to use but doesn't have the precision of a Parametric or FFT effect. For general EQ tasks choose the 10 Band (1 octave) or 20 Band (1/2 octave) equalizer. Tasks requiring a finer degree of control use the 30 Band (1/3 Octave) equalizer.

When equalising low frequencies raise the value of the accuracy control to between 500 and 5000 points. Higher frequencies require less accuracy and therefore less processing time. Lower values in the accuracy dialog reduce the amount of CPU time taken to process this effect. Extend the range of the sliders using the range control between 40 to 180db. This is way beyond the capability of hardware units. Graphic equalisers may be used in the effects racks although for greater control use only 1 or 1/2 octaves and lower accuracy values.

Graphical Phase Shifter

The Graphic Phase shifter enables phase to be controlled over time by the use of the graph. Click to place handles on the graph and move the handles around the graph to produce phase shifting at those points. The Phase Shifter isn't an 'effect' as much as a process audio solution. For instance the Phase Shifter can produce simulated stereo effects. Use the marquee selection tool in the Spectral Frequency View to select parts of the frequency only. For instance select just the upper frequencies and phase shift 180 degrees against the lower frequencies. The effect will not be heard if the phase shifter effect is used on both channels. This is because both channels will still be in phase. To hear the effect, use the effect one channel only by selecting from the channel options in the Graphic Phase Shifter dialogue.

Notch Filter

Notch Filtering enables control of precise frequencies without affecting other neighbouring frequencies. It is used for removing or identifying noise or tones within a waveform. Up to six frequencies may be affected in one pass. Enable editing by placing a check mark in one of the 'Tones To Notch' boxes and enter the frequency in Hz. Enter a positive or a negative value in the attenuation box. Choosing Super Narrow from the Width options will only affect the single frequencies specified in the dialog. Use the presets in this effect when removing electrical or radio interference from recordings. The Notch Filter is able to remove just the selected frequencies without affecting any other and is very useful in forensic and scientific restoration.

Parametric Equaliser

The Parametric EQ effect enables the creation of measurable controls such as the selection of a frequency band and the application of those controls to the range or waveform. This EQ effect provides the ability to create controls over just certain areas of the waveform. In this way it is different from EQ effects such as the Graphic EQ which allow control over pre-set frequency bands.

The effect window contains a graph which showing Frequency on the X axis and Amplitude on the Y Axis. Underneath the graph are five sweepable frequency controls and on the right of the graph is the same number of amplitude controls. Check marks next to each frequency control enable or

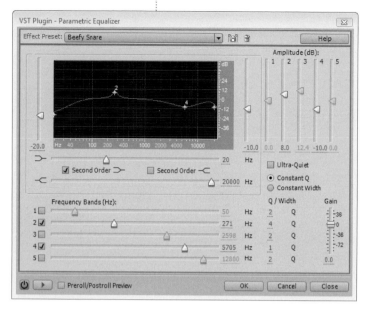

disable that control. Use this effect when you need to apply a number of EQ decisions over the audio in a single process. For instance a 2nd Order High Pass filter with a dip at 400Hz and a slight .2dB boost at 1200Hz can be applied at the same time.

Operation is very simple; Enable a centre frequency by placing a checkmark against any unused frequency control and drag the fader to adjust the frequency in Hz. Alternatively click on the figure and overtype to manually enter a value in the dialog. Enabling a centre frequency also enables an amplitude slider to the right of the frequency plot. Produce a 10dB boost over the centre frequency and sweep the frequency up and down until resonant frequencies in the track stand out. Use the Q control to widen or narrow the affected band of frequencies by using larger or smaller numbers respectively. Apply high or low shelving using the Cutoff and Level controls under and to the left and right of the graph, For instance; create a high pass filter using a 2nd order Low Shelf at around 100Hz with around -40dB of attenuation,

Although the faders have a great deal of travel, the most useful part of the fader is between 0 and -6dB. Avoid extremes of EQ cut and boost unless you want a very unnatural sound. Likewise very high Q values can create ringing tones. Use Q values of around 10 for general EQ.

Tip

Values adjusted using the X (centre frequency) and Y (amplitude) slider are shown on the plot in real time. Click over the small dots in the lot and drag to new locations for an alternative method of editing.

Quick Filter

Envelope filter like effects can be produced with the 'Quick Filter' transform. This transform enables varying tone control over time (like using the EQ control on a mixer as the track is playing) – instead of a fixed frequency adjustment, or broad EQ curve applied to the waveform as a whole. The effect is subtle over time but the Quick Filter tool is powerful as each fader is a centre frequency for a bell curve so boosting 7.3kHz is pushing frequencies around that centre frequency too. For example to produce a 'Waves on shingle' white noise sound;

1 Create about 12 seconds of white noise using Generate, Noise.
2 Select the entire waveform and remove the checkmark in 'Lock to these settings only'.

3 On the first page boost 86,172,689, 7.3 and 22k by about 20%.
4 On the Final Settings page drop the same bands by about 30%. You'll hear a bass and treble boost gradually diminishing towards the end of the noise sample.
5 Create 'pulsing' effects using a short white noise sample (.5 secs) and extreme quick filter settings.
6 Insert the wave into the multitrack and duplicate as necessary or simple copy and merge paste into one waveform several times.

Scientific Filters (Process)
Scientific Filters apply high-order IIR (Infinite Impulse Response) filters over the waveform or range. Four common types of high order filter are available; Bessel, Butterworth, Chebychev (Chebyshev) 1and 2. Of these scientific types of filter the Butterworth often provides the maximum trade off between frequency and roll off attenuation.

Restoration Effects
Restoration effects include the click and pop eliminator and the noise reduction tool. Adobe Audition 2.0 restoration effects are used for removing background noise from recordings, scratches from vinyl recordings and hiss from radio broadcasts recordings.

Auto Click Pop Eliminator (Process)
The Auto Click / Pop Eliminator is a useful tool for simple removal of pops and clicks. Importantly this effect offers a preview function so the results can be heard immediately.

Click & Pop Eliminator
The Click and Pop Eliminator is an archiving tool created for the easy removal of clicks, pops and scratches from a recording made of an old and damaged vinyl (or any other material) LP. The process is as simple as making a waveform of the source material and choosing Effects,Noise Reduction,Click and Pop Eliminator from the menu bar. Within the dialog box press the Auto Find All Levels button to scan and detect clicks and pops within the waveform. This effect doesn't offer a preview function and the process of scanning the waveform can be lengthy, especially when applied over a long section of audio. For this reason select a typically noisy section to experiment with and when happy with your results save this as a preset (just in case of accidents)

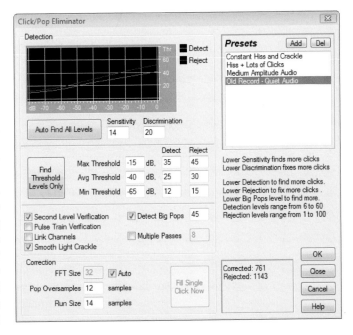

before applying the transform over the entire length of the recording. The results are spectacular and when combined with a little multi-band compression can completely rejuvenate an old and abused LP. For best results always convert 16bit files to 32bit before applying the Click and Pop Eliminator. Best practise is to work wholly in the 32bit domain and only downsample to 16bit if mastering to CD or preparing the waveform for distribution.

Clip Restoration (Process)

Clipping is the noise that occurs when the analogue input levels seen by the ADC (Analogue Digital Convertor) of a soundcard or digital device are higher than the converters ability to mathematically convert that level into sample data. This is shown in the waveform view as a flattened shape at the top of the wave. This is reproduced as noise.

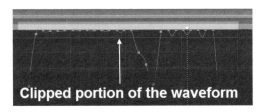

Clipped portion of the waveform

Clipping happens in one of two ways; either as a result of too much level into your sound card from wrongly adjusted external equipment, or by over amplification of a waveform. Clipped portions of a waveform are recognisable by being 'chopped off' at the top and bottom and are heard as a distorted sound. If areas of a waveform have become clipped during recording and if the recording cannot be made again such as a live recording it is possible to repair the damaged waveform and reduce the effects of clipping. Convert the file to a 32bit file if not done already and select the entire clipped waveform, including the clipped areas. Apply the Clip Restoration effect with no attenuation then apply the Hard Limiting effect with no boost and a –0.2dB limit.

Hiss Reduction (Process)

Just as the Pop and Click Eliminator can help when archiving and mastering from vinyl, the Hiss Reduction 'effect' can remove hiss from noisy tape recordings. The results are not as spectacular as with the Click reduction, especially when the music or speech on the tape is only a little more audible than the hiss. But it's still the best tool around for the job. Start as usual by recording the source audio to a 32bit waveform if not done already. Apply the Hiss Reduction tool (Effects, Restoration, Hiss Reduction) to a typically noisy area of the wave and experiment within the dialog to produce the best results. The Hiss Reduction tool is best applied sparingly. An attempt to remove absolutely all evidence of the hiss will result in a 'squelched' sound as portions of the desired information are removed along with the hiss. When selecting audio for analysis before applying the effect try and choose an area of the audio that has no music or speech present and also an area that has a smaller amount of high frequency information. See the comprehensive help files for detailed information on this effect.

Tip

For best results when recording into Adobe Audition use 32bit resolution and leave -6db of headroom between the highest amplitude and 0dBf.

Noise Reduction (Process)

Use noise reduction any time that the foreground sound is obscured partially by a wide frequency background noise. For example; you have recorded a soft piano piece for an examination but the recording is spoilt by an unnoticed fan heater in the room. The noise is only apparent when you listen back.

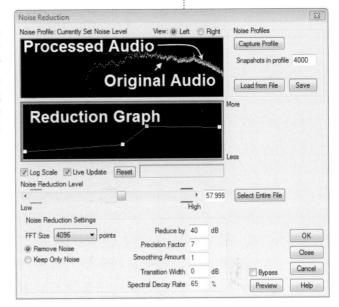

1 If necessary convert the waveform to 32bit.
2 Select any area of the waveform which contains as much of the background noise (in this case the heater) as possible.
3 Once a suitably 'noisy' area has been selected use the Capture Noise Reduction Profile Tool (Effects, Restoration menu) to capture the noise profile of that selection.
4 Choose Effects.Restoration,Noise Reduction from the menu. The noise profile is loaded into the tool and shown in the upper graph. The original signal is shown as a line of yellow dots, the red line of dots is the processed audio and the green area is the noise floor.
5 Place handles in the area where the noise profile is strongest and create a curve which will not apply the noise reduction to areas of the frequency where noise is not a problem.
6 Use the noise reduction level fader to reduce the amount of reduction. Artifacts will appear in the audio If the fader is left at its maximum. The intention is to use the minimum amount of reduction and only to use it in areas where the noise is more apparent. Use the preview feature to hear the reduction in real time.
7 Choose a Snapshot value of 64 and an FFT Size of 4096. Change the 'Reduce By' value to 40db, the Precision Factor to 7 and the Smoothing Amount to 2.

If the noise reduction doesn't appear to be affecting the troublesome frequencies raise the FFT Size to 6000 or more and experiment with other values.

When the maximum balance between noise and noise reduction has been achieved click over the button 'Select Entire File'. The range is extended to the entire waveform. Press OK to apply the Noise Reduction over the wave.

The noise reduction dialog contains many options for further enhancing the noise reduction effect. The first thing to do is establish whether there is too much noise reduction. Drag the Noise Reduction Level slider from right to left. The Graph at the top of the screen will change to show a red line where the current selection is and a yellow line illustrating the noise reduc-tion. Maximum noise reduction can easily disturb parts of the wave that you want to keep. Experiment with values around 90% or less to retain as much of the musical quality of the piece as possible. Use the 'Keep Only Noise' option to establish how much of the foreground noise is missing. FFT (Fast Fourier Transform) Size determines the resolution (in frequency bands) of the transform. Experiment with values from 4096 to 12000 depending on the nature of the material and the intensity of the background noise. If the noise profile is louder in certain frequency ranges use the reduction graph to lessen the effect of the noise profile in the un-affected frequency ranges. If the fan heater is on a wooden floor it may produce unwanted noise only in the frequency range 100 – 200 Hz. To apply noise reduction in this range only click on the reduction graph to create a node and drag the node on the extreme right to the bottom of the graph. This lessens the effect of the noise reduction profile in the upper frequencies.

Quote

A dramatic increase in performance can be achieved by capturing the noise reduction profile over a few seconds of silence before the audio starts. Apply this profile over the entire waveform before applying further effects.

Special Effects

Convolution (Process)

Convolution is the tool to use when you don't happen to have the cash to hire St Pauls Cathedral for your Xmas Choir or if you'd enjoy hearing a rock guitar solo in the British Library. Convolution is also the technique employed to produce stunningly realistic 'modeller' amps and effects. It works because if the samples in one waveform are multiplied with the samples in another the target waveform will adopt the characteristics of the source. In practice this means that an impulse file of a reverberating space (such as the inside of a lift or a huge cathedral) can be imposed on a suitable sound. The effect is to place the sound inside the reverberating space. Literally, using this technique it is possible to put your lead vocalist in La Scala. More realistically convolution is the way to apply the sound of that all important mike or reverb to a waveform. In other words your guitar or vocal can appear to have been treated with the most impossibly expensive reverb or recorded with the best microphones. Of course it's not as easy as all that. Convolution needs two waveforms; the source (your original recording) and the impulse (the sound of the effect). Finding impulse files can be tricky and most people make up their own. But if you can beg or borrow some equipment for a day or so, it's easy to make your own.

A basic impulse file may be created as follows:

1 Close all waves (and sessions if using Adobe Audition 1.0).
2 Choose Generate,Silence from the menu bar.
3 Generate 5 seconds of silence.
4 At the New Waveform dialog choose 44100, mono, 32bit file.
5 Using the Zoom selection tool zoom right into the very start of the new waveform until the individual samples appear as small squares.
6 Double click on the first one and enter 32000 as a value.
7 Return to view the whole waveform.

8 Apply a reverb effect over the whole wave (choose a full, smooth reverb with a long tail in this instance).

9 Drag Select over the reverb impulse taking care to include the whole of the tail.

10 Choose Effects>Special>Convolution.

11 Press 'Clear'.

12 In the Scaled By field enter 100.

13 Press 'Add Sel'.

14 Press 'Save' to save the new impulse.

15 Press 'Close'.

Applying your impulse:

1 Load any waveform.

2 Choose Effect,Special,Convolution.

3 Load your saved impulse (if not already loaded).

4 Press OK.

At first you'll find that the effect sounds not as expected. Experiment with differing values and reverbs etc. Also try experimenting with filters and delay. Most dynamic effects (Compression, distortion etc.) don't suit convolution.

Distortion

Don't be tempted to see the Distortion effect as a substitute for your Turbo Rat or Big Muff guitar effects pedal. This distortion is much better used as a 'grungeliser' to mess up your waveforms in the sickest way possible. It does contain some interesting features such as the interesting ability to apply separate distortion values for positive numbers (above the green centre line in waveform view) and negative numbers (below the green line). Simply uncheck the 'symmetrical' box in the Distortion effects dialog to choose this option. The Distortion effect is also great when producing 'lo-fi' sounds or creating retro mixes.

1 Load your mix.

2 Apply a –25db 'brickwall' limiter.

3 Apply the Bow Curve 1 distortion effect.

Time and Pitch effects

Doppler Shifter (Process)

Use the Doppler Shift effect whenever you need to simulate a car or plane passing by. The effect will work on both mono and stereo waveforms although the effect is much more apparent with stereo waveforms. Briefly the Doppler Effect occurs as waves of moving air reach the ear with more or less frequency depending on whether the source (car or train, etc.) is moving towards you, or away from you. The effect is an ascending or descending shift in pitch. The effect combines pitch shift with panning to create the illusion of movement. To illustrate this we can create the noise of a jet fighter passing low overhead at an air show.

Tip

Convolution may be used to apply a Reverb, EQ and Delay set over a waveform. Apply the effects in turn to the test impulse and save.

1 Create a stereo 32bit waveform containing 10 seconds of pink noise.
2 Use the Dynamic Delay to create the illusion of screaming engine noise by creating a diagonal line from left to right with values of 0.50ms at the left and 4ms at the right.
3 Use the Doppler Shifter to create a dramatic illusion of movement using the following values; Starting Distance Away: 1500, Velocity:355, Coming From:270, Passes In Front: 75, Passes On Right: 0.

Finally press the Preview button to hear the effect of the Doppler Shifter on the white noise.

Pitch Bender (Process)

The Pitch Bender effect applies pitch effects over time. This is not a pitch correction or resampling effect but it is very useful for special effects particularly over voices. The Pitch Bender effect is shown as a curve on the graph, The centre line is no change, up is pitch up and down is pitch down. Place handles on the graph and drag to create pitch bending effects. Right click over any handle to see the value or click and drag off the screen to remove. The most dramatic effects from this effect come from experimenting with the Range values, particularly selecting the BPM option and using values of 90BPM over a base of around 50BPM. To create the illusion that your recording is of a multitrack tape select the first second of the recording and create two nodes at the very left hand side of the graph with the following values:

	Time Index	Pitch
Node1	0	6.11
Node2	0.01	7.06

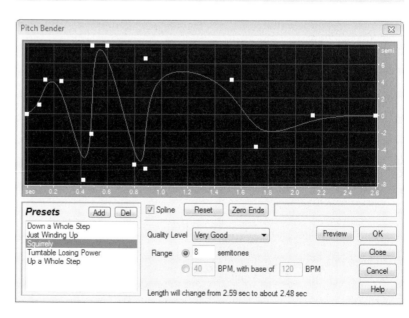

The remainder of the graph should be completely flat. This very small pitch change gives the impression of the reel of tape snatching up to speed, characteristic of the behaviour of a multitrack tape.

The range control in this dialog enables the X Axis to display either semitones or BPM (Beats Per Minute). To raise or lower the BPM of a breakbeat or loop:

1 Load the waveform containing the loop and choose Effects>Time/Pitch>Pitch Bender.
2 Ensure the graph is 'flat' and select the BPM range option.
3 Replace the default value in the BPM range field with 100 BPM and if possible enter the original tempo of the loop into the 'base of' field although this isn't entirely necessary and won't affect the result. However if your target tempo is critical this value will need to be entered correctly to enable the program to calculate the desired tempo.
4 Right click on the first and last nodes in the graph to manually enter a target tempo.

The Pitch Shifter effect can only change tempo by raising or lowering pitch, it is unable to 'recycle' or change tempo without affecting the sound of the instruments.

Pitch Correction (Process)

Pitch correction is used to Auto-Tune or Pitch Quantize solo melodic passages. It is intended for vocals although could be used on any waveform with the same qualities.

The Pitch Correction effect has two modes; Automatic and Manual. In Automatic mode the correct pitch is calculated from scale information and the audio is corrected. A vertical graph on the right side of the effect indicates the level of correction.

1 Load a mono or stereo waveform into the edit view and choose a reference channel. The reference channel should have the strongest signal and be more accurate in pitch
2 Choose the Pitch Correction effect from the effects menu and if necessary change the reference channel from the default at the top of the window.
3 If the Scale is set at chromatic, the effect will attempt to simply correct the note by rounding up or down to the nearest half step. If the Minor or Major scale is used, the effect will attempt to correct

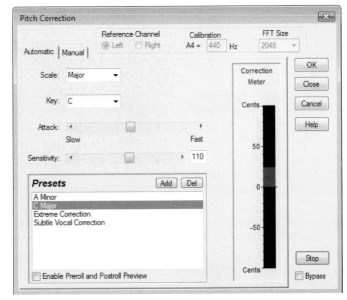

to the nearest note on the scale. Chromatic changes are more subtle than changes decided on scale.

4   Choose attack and sensitivity depending on the nature of the waveform. At extreme settings this will produce Vocoder like effects.

5   Preview the effect using preroll if necessary

In manual mode the Pitch Correction effect can be tuned to the characteristics of the source audio. This process is not automatic and is too lengthy for everything other than wild excursions away from the note but can be a useful restoration tool.

1   Load a mono or stereo waveform and establish the reference channel

2   The pitch correction effect analyses the waveform and shows pitch information in the upper graph and amplitude information in the lower graph. The green range bar in the middle can be adjusted to zoom in on certain parts of the waveform. Click and drag at either end of the range bar to adjust.

3   In the pitch reference graph the red line is the source audio and the green line is the adjustable pitch. Clicking and dragging on the blue centre line causes the green line to move above or below the red line. When the line is above the red line the corrected audio has a higher pitch than the original. When the green line is below the red lie the corrected audio has a lower pitch.

4   Carefully drag the blue line along above and below the centre line to correct intonation problems in the source audio. If the singer appears to be singing flat, move the green line above the red line and vice versa.

The manual pitch corrector produces a much more natural result than the automatic corrector but takes significantly more time. The automatic correc-

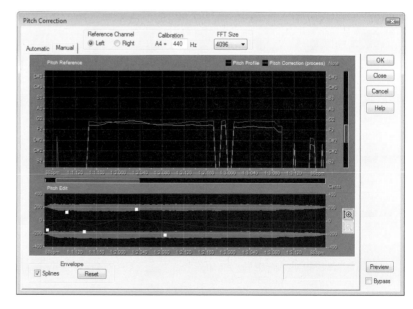

tor laid over backing vocal parts manages to correct minor intonation problems. Neither of these effects can be used in the effects rack or in the mastering effects.

Pitch Shifter

Simple pitch shifting effects can be produced using the Pitch Shifter Stretch effect which is a VST effect and so can be used in effects racks and automated. The accuracy of the Pitch Shifting effect isn't great enough for use as a vocal corrector. Use the Pitch Shifter effect for creative effects such as harmonizing effects or special voices.

Stretch

The Time Stretch effect creates 'Recycle' style accurate pitch shifting for correcting bum notes or bringing drum loops into time. Waveforms may be shifted in pitch, in time without affecting pitch or resampled in which case both time and pitch is affected. The depth of the pitch effect or the speed of the effect is both adjusted by the large horizontal slider bar in the middle of the dialog. Move the bar to the left to slow tempo or to the right to speed up. Confusingly moving the bar to the left raises the pitch while moving it to the right lowers pitch.

Quote

When using the Time Stretch effect always enter 100 in the Ratio box as a default value. This value is not the starting BPM of the loop, it is the ratio by which the sample will be stretched. A value of 100 means 'no change', lower or higher numbers mean the sample will be stretched or shrunk appropriately.

In cases where a whole track must be adjusted (perhaps the guitar player was out of time or the singer requires a different key) experiment with chopping the waveform into smaller more manageable pieces in order to perform the task.

It is possible to permanently change the tempo of a loop in BPM using the Pitch Shifter effect after calculating the original BPM of the loop using Edit>Edit Tempo. The pitch (sound) of the loop at the new tempo can then be raised or lowered in pitch using the Stretch tool to preserve the new tempo.

To varispeed bum notes or phrases choose 'Pitch Shift' to keep the crucial timing intact. The Transpose drop down box provides almost an octave of preset transpositions from 11b (flat) to 11# (sharp) these values have no effect when the 'Preserve Pitch' option is chosen. The third option 'Resample' changes both pitch and length depending on the ratio chosen. Choose the Low Precision option in multitrack view and while previewing. In Edit view choose High Precision (which takes much longer) while applying the effect when you are happy that everything is going to be OK. Advanced users may choose to apply particular values in the Splicing Frequency and Overlapping boxes. If you aren't sure about the values (and don't have a couple of days to experiment) put a check mark in the 'Choose Appropriate Defaults' box to allow the program to make a fairly accurate (better than mine anyway) guess. The second page of the Stretch effect dialog enables the Stretch effect to produce gliding Pitch Bender style effects.

Quote

Pressing F2 on the keyboard re-applies the last used effect with the same parameters. This can be useful when applying an effect over portions of a waveform without revisiting the effects dialog or the need to create a new item in the favourites menu.

The Generate Menu

Effects are used to process samples. The list of tools in the Generate menu will each create new samples in an empty waveform.

Silence (Process)

Does what it says on the tin. Creates enough zero amplitude samples to fill a required space. Very useful for adding silence at the end of the waveform when space is needed to carry a reverb tail etc.

DTMF (Process)

Dial Tone Multi Frequency tones are used in key pad telephony. The tones are interpreted at the telephone company and used to decide how the call is to be directed. They can be used scientifically, for generating auto diallers etc. Or they can be used creatively.

Noise (Process)

Adobe Audition generates noise by creating samples with random amplitude and frequency values. Samples are spread equally over the frequency and amplitude spectrum. Brown noise contains more frequencies in the lower end of the spectrum. Pink noise contains frequencies in the middle range. White noise is a true random selection of frequencies spread over the spectrum. White noise also occurs in nature. Surf sounds, heavy rain and waterfall sounds are all examples of natural white noise.

Tones (Process)

Tones created at specific frequencies are heard as music. The tone generator can be used to create scientific tones such as used in audio analysis or to produce tones for scientific applications such as test tones.

The Generate Tones tool can be used to modulate the tones with the underlying waveform. This is fantastic for creating spooky effects. Try modulating a rising tone over brown or pink noise.

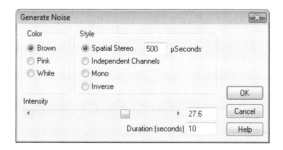

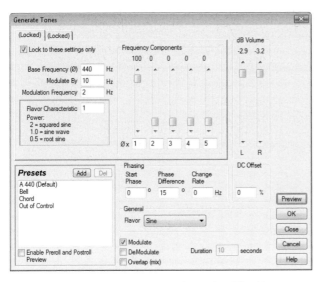

1 Create a new wave in the edit view using File, New.
2 Copy the settings in this picture to the Generate Noise dialogue (above).
3 Copy the settings in this picture to the Generate Tones dialogue.

Add some reverb or some phasing over the result to create a sinister bed.

Favourites

After a while of working with Adobe Audition you'll find a workflow that
suits you. Very often this will include a number of processes which are
regularly used. Adobe Audition contains a convenient way of storing
and recalling these often used processes in the Favorites menu. Along
side the custom favorites are a number of factory pre-set favorites;
Choose favorites from the Favorites menu. Favorites are destructive
and can only be used in the edit view.

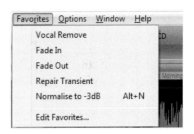

Vocal Remove	Uses the Centre Channel Extractor effect to remove information from the centre of a stereo panorama. In commercial music the lead vocal or feature parts are usually panned dead centre. Using the Centre Channel Extractor over this audio will remove some or all of the vocal depending on how the audio was produced.
Fade In	Is an application of the Amplitude/Envelope (Process) effect. Produces an envelope curve over a range set over the beginning of the waveform.
Fade Out	Another Amplitude / Envelope curve. Creates a gradual fade out over a range set over the end of a waveform.
Repair Transient	A transient is a very high and very fast peak which may not be described by the level meters. Transients can be produced by cymbal crashes or excessive vocal sibilance. Transients are heard as pops or clicks. This favorite uses the Restoration/Click Pop Eliminator effect to reduce the effect of transients as far as possible.

Normalize to -3dB Is an application of the Amplitude/Normalize effect. Reduces the amplitude of the waveform or range by -3dB. In the logarithmic scale this is an apparent halving of the amplitude.

Edit Favorites

Favourites are either favourite effect settings or scripts. A script is a small computer program that can run through a set of actions (open file, process with an effect, close file) without user intervention.

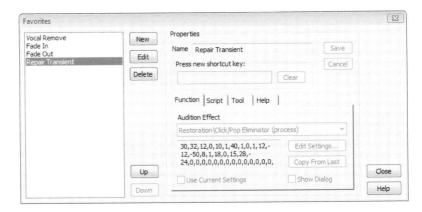

Creating a favorite effect

Create a a shortcut that will normalise a file to −3dB.

1 In the Edit Menu choose Favourites>Edit Favourites from the main menu bar.
2 Press New and enter Normalise to −3dB in the Name property box.
3 Click once in the shortcut property box, press and hold the Alt key on the keyboard and tap the N key once. Alt+N will appear in the shortcut box as your keystroke to invoke this shortcut. If the key is already assigned to another function you will receive a notification at this point.
4 Choose the Function tab and navigate the drop down list until you find Amplitude\Normalize (process).

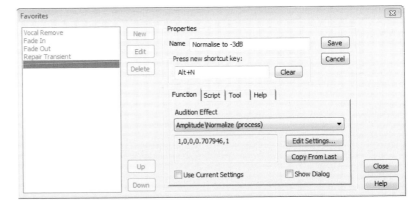

5   Press the Edit Settings box and set the normalize parameters to −3dB
    equally. Press OK to return to the Favorites dialog.
6   Make sure that the Show Dialog box is not checked.
7   Press Save to save this as a favourite.

The option to use current settings will remove the preset settings and process the range or waveform with the current settings for that effect. This is
useful if you have a particular EQ to be applied over several places in the
waveform. Or choose Copy from Last to copy the current settings into the
favorite.

    Now whenever you are in the edit view you may normalise any file to −3dB
simply by pressing Alt+N. Favourites may also be made to invoke other programs. For instance a script can be created which could save the current
selection as an Mp3 file. Another favorite could then be created which would
invoke an Mp3 player with the filename as the argument.

Scripts and Batch Processing

Scripting enables repetitive tasks to be automated. This includes applying
effects and saving waveforms. In the creation of the script file actions and
menu operations are recorded. Range selections are recorded but mouse
movements are not. The resulting script file (.scp) is a plain text file which
can be edited using a simple text editor such as notepad. Batch processing
enables a script to be applied over a number of files and then enables the
files to be saved by the program. In this way large numbers of waveforms can
be processed very quickly.

    For example; you have recorded one side of an LP for archiving. You have
created cue ranges for each song on the LP and would like to apply click and
pop elimination and normalizing to each song. A script that uses the currently selected range can be created to easily automate this task. Scripts can
also be made to work with no waveform loaded (in which case the script must
open a wave file), or to work on the whole currently loaded waveform. NB
This procedure assumes that you have created a waveform containing the
songs from one side of your LP and that you have created named marker
ranges for each song.

Creating a script from scratch for a cue range or song

1   Open the Marker window (Alt + 8) and double click on the first item in
    the Cue List, which should be your first song. The cue range is now
    highlighted.
2   Choose File, Scripts. Push the 'Open/New Collection' and choose a place
    to store your script and a name for the script collection. This can be a
    different name from the action of the script. For instance if you plan to
    make a few scripts to use when restoring vinyl you may choose 'Vinyl
    Toolkit' as a collection name.
3   Click over the 'Open/New Collection' button.
4   Type a descriptive name for this new de-clicker and normalize script in
    the Title dialog.
5   Push 'record'. From this point on the software will record your actions.

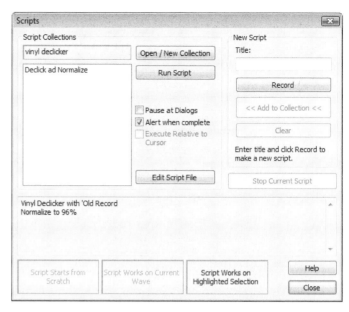

Now edit the selected range as normal.

6 Choose Effects, Restoration, Click and Pop Eliminator (Process) and apply the Old Record preset.

7 When finished, choose Effects>Amplitude>Normalize(Process) and normalize the selected range to 96%.

8 When the effects have been applied return to File, Scripts and push the 'Stop Current Script' button.

9 Type a short helpful description for the script including reminders of presets and values used if you like. Choose 'Add To Collection'. The title of the script appears in the collections list.

10 Press 'Close'.

This script can now be used as a tool for each of the cue ranges in your wave-form.

1 Return to the Cue List and double click the second song in the list.

2 Choose File, Scripts, Adobe Audition remembers the open collection and we can see our script title in the left hand window. Remember to remove the check mark from the option 'Pause At Dialogs' or you'll need to sit in front of the computer and press 'OK' to agree to every effect!

3 Click on the title of the script and press 'Run Script'.

4 The script runs and transforms our second song with no need for input.

This is great as far as it goes but it's not completely automatic. The only way to select another range is to return to the computer after the script has run. What's needed is a way to edit all the songs, one at a time with no need for user input. Using the batch function in the Marker Window, we can save each song as a different file. The batch processor can then run the Declick and Normalize script on each of the saved tracks.

Batch Processing

It's normal when manipulating audio to find yourself repeating the same task on a number of waveforms. For instance; when preparing jingles for a radio show you need to normalise and apply a little balance EQ to a waveform before saving as an mp3 for sending over the network. This is a complex

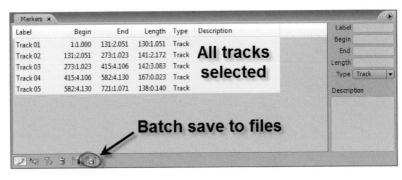

task for just one waveform. But the station as just bought 50 new station idents and they all need to be prepped for that evenings launch. That could take hours without some automation. Batch processing enables you to choose which scripts to use over which files and then automates that process. The following section will walk you through this problem.

The radio station has placed a collection of jingles in a folder for processing.

1 In the edit view, choose 'Batch Processing' from the File Menu
2 In the first Tab choose Add files to place all the jingles in the list of files for processing
3 In the second tab select 'run Script' and browse to the script collection library that contains the script you need to run over the files.
4 In the New Format tab choose the output format for the files
5 In the destination tab choose the target folder for the new mp3 files.

Batch processing loads, processes and saves each file in turn.

Sharing and manually editing script files

As well as saving time now, scripts can be shared with other Adobe Audition users. Scripts are stored in easily understandable plain text files (*.scp). Script files can be copied, pasted or otherwise manipulated just like any other text document and saved anywhere. To manually edit a script from within the Scripts and Batch Processing dialog box push the 'Edit Script File' button. This causes Windows Notepad to open with the contents of the current script file. Otherwise simply open script file with Notepad.

Renaming a script

Every collection is simply called 'New Collection' when created. Rename the collection by editing the text after the colon: in the first line of the script file. The new title is now seen whenever the script file is loaded.

```
batch utilties.scp

!Collection title. Time to edit that spelling?

Collection: Batch Utilites

!Plain Text title;

Title: Normalize to -0.3dB

!The following lines appear in the description panel

Description: This script is used to normalize files to -0.3dB.  It can be run on a
single file or batch processed on multiple files.
Description: Single File:  Open the file, select this script, and click 'Run Script'.
Description: Multiple Files:  Go to File>Batch Processing to run this script on mul-
tiple files.  In step 1, you add the files you want to convert, and in step 2 you can
choose this script. Click the Help button in the batch processing dialog for more
help.

!Mode 2 is Script Works on Current Wave

Mode: 2

!Range, Frequency and Channel selections

Selected: none at 0 scaled 3987816 SR 44100
Freq: Off
        cmd: Channel Both

        Selected: 0 to 3987814 scaled 3987816 SR 44100
        Freq: Off

!Load the Normalize effect with the following parameters

        Comment: Amplitude\Normalize
        cmd: {7EC45406-CFB6-4C54-99B9-84CE080C1914}
        1: 1
        2: 0
        3: 0
        4: 0.966051
        5: 1

        Freq: Off
        End:
```

Adobe Audition is supplied with three example scripts in C:\Program Files\Adobe\Adobe Audition 2.0\Scripts. Load any script into Notepad.

Tip

If your system partition or disk suffers a failure you can always reinstall the software. But any scripts you make will be lost. If you can, always choose another partition or disk to for your personal data.

Saving and Exporting

Finished waveforms in the edit view can be exported into other applications, saved in a number of file formats and imported into the multitrack view.

When you need to:	Do this:
Save a changed file normally after working for a while and making valuable changes	File,Save
Save a changed file without saving over the original	File,Save As. Give the new file a name
Save a changed file without saving over the original and continue to work on the original *	File, Save Copy As. Give the new copy a name.
Save just the contents of a range.	File,Save Selection. Give the new file a name.
Save all changed files over the original files.	File,Save All
Ditch all changes to the currently loaded waveform and start again.	File,Revert To Saved.

* when a file is saved using 'Save As' the original is closed and the new copy is loaded. When a file is saved used 'Save Copy As' the new copy is not loaded into the workspace. This is the command to use when you want to save changes to a copy of the file but continue to work on the original.

Non Audio Information

Adobe Audition 2.0 has been developed with the production of audio for broadcast and digital distribution in mind. For this reason it is able to save many types of standard information along with the audio file information. RIFF chunk data and other data may be stored in files saved in linear PCM WAV format. In addition, track information may be stored for use by digital file players, radio cart software and samplers. Not all file formats can save non-audio information. Adobe Audition 2.0 does not include tools for Digital Rights Management (copy prevention).

WAV non-audio information

Adobe Audition can save information in one of three formats within a WAV file.

Standard RIFF	Resource Interchange File Format information.
Radio Industry	Broadcast Radio information. Commercial information.
MP3 (ID3 Tag)	ID3v2.3-compatible information.

To encode information in this way, the correct selection must be made from the menu at the top of the File Info dialogue box in the Text Fields tab. Once saved with the file, the information remains with the file for its lifetime.The following data may also be encoded:

BWF	Broadcast Wave File	Data chunks containing information required for the EBU standard.
Cart	Cart Information	Data containing information used by radio industry cart programs
Bitmap	Picture Information	

Broadcast Wave Standards

Broadcast wave file standards are a development by the EBU (European Broadcast Union) of the standard wave file format. The BWF enabled wav is able to contain meta information which the standard WAV file cannot. Adobe Audition 2.0 encodes this additional data if the option to save Broadcast Wave Data is selected in the BWF tab of the File Info dialogue. When a WAV file contains BWF data it is known as a BWF file although the file extension remains the same.

Quote

The EBU standard for BWF files is to use the .wav file extension. This is to provide the maximum capability with audio equipment. The standard also defines the audio format as 'linear PCM, 16 bits, sampled at 48 kHz'. Files sampled at 44.1kHz are allowed but the specification notes that you can't expect anyone to play them!

Text Fields Tab (Standard RIFF)

Display Title
Original Artist
Name
Genre
Key Words
Digitization Source
Original Medium
Engineers
Digitizer
Source Supplier
Copyright
Software Package *
Creation Date *
Comments
Subject

Text Fields Tab (Radio Industry)

Description
Advertiser
Outcue
Start Date
End Date
Intro Time (ms/begin)
Sec Tone (ms/end)
Producer
Talent
Category
Agency
Account Executive
Creation Date *
Comments
Copy

Text Fields Tab (MP3 ID3 Tag)

Song Title
Artist
Album Name
Genre
Year *
Comments
Track Number

Loop Info

Loop information required for the multitrack is prepared in this section. Only simple loop options are enabled for a waveform in the multitrack view unless the loop is prepared in the edit view. The tempo and key of the loop are entered here along with the tempo matching option for this waveform. Settings in this dialogue are for the entire waveform. If loops have been created using ranges in the waveform all those ranges have the same loop options. When creating multiple loops from a single waveform the ranges must each be saved as a new file and loop options set individually for each file.

Sampler

Sample information is saved in the header of the .WAV file.

Target Manufacturer. This field is not editable. Contains data created by external sampler when writing .wav if available.
Target product Code. This field is not editable. Contains data created by external sampler when writing .wav if available.

Sample Period. The sample rate is shown in this field. This is editable if you wish the target sampler to reproduce data at a different rate.

MIDI Unity Note is where data enabling the host device to map the sample to the correct key or MIDI note is stored. If the sample is a musical one the Note value should be set to the unity note of the waveform (Adobe Audition will analyse and detect this if necessary). Use the Fine Tune function to bring the note exactly into tune.

The SMPTE offset section is where SMPTE information for that waveform is stored. Set the SMPTE format and offset values to suit your environment.

Sampler loops

Sampler Loops are used by compatible hardware and software samplers. Sampler Loops appear in the Marker window and the File Panel but Markers are not automatically added to the Loop information. Loops have differing attributes such as Infinite Looping, number of loops, direction, etc. To create a loop and add it to the sampler information.

1   Create a seamless looping range within the waveform.
2   Right click over the waveform and choose File Info from the menu.
3   In the Sampler tab choose the option to save Sampler information and click over the 'New' button to add the loop to the list and set attributes accordingly.

Miscellaneous

These are legacy options unused by nearly all audio players. The bitmap option encodes a tiny 32 x 32 bmp into the file header which some systems can use in file properties. The picture entered here is not the album art that appears when a wma file is played in the Windows Media Player. Wma album art is a tag that is encoded within the Media Player itself. Within Windows Media Player. Right click over any file and choose Advanced Tags to see album art properties.

Broadcast Wave

BWF information from this section is encoded into the wav file along with audio information. A properly encoded file containing BWF data can then be

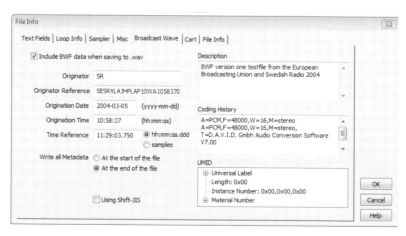

shared or distributed among broadcasters and each broadcaster will receive the information along with the file.

A great deal of information about the BWF standard and the file downloaded for this grab can be found at the following URL;

http://www.sr.se/utveckling/tu/bwf/

Cart Chunk Info

Cart Chunk data (AES46-2002) is a labelling system for the radio industry. Information provided in cart chunk form enables the broadcast industry to identify and quickly incorporate waveforms using proprietary equipment and systems. Cart data also contains maker and range data enabling the broadcaster to simply import and use a waveform in a broadcast with little or no preparation. More information can be found at www.cartchunk.org.

File Info

Non editable file information about the waveform is presented in this section.

XMP Info

Extensible Metadata Platform data is stored with WAV, mp3 or CEL data and can be read by any application that supports XMP. All Adobe applications support this encoding. XMP data is also written to files in the Adobe Bridge. XMP data is not visible in Adobe Audition 2.0 unless the File Info dialogue is produced.

The CD view

Use the CD view toggle on the menu bar or press Shift + F12 to switch to the CD view. The CD view is where audio waveforms are compiled into a CD list in preparation for burning to CD. Currently Adobe Audition does not have the ability to burn to DVD or to create multisession CD's.

Compiling a CD from imported waveforms

I want to re create a Beatles album using a collection of Beatles songs ripped from the original album using Windows Media Player. The songs are in WMA format.

1 Open the files using File, Open from the Menu bar. Remember to choose the option to open files of type; .wma or the files won't be visible when you browse for them.
2 The files appear in the files panel ordered sequentially, with numbers beginning with 1 at the top and 0 at the bottom. This doesn't matter as the tracks will be re-ordered in my new CD.
3 Drag each file onto the main CD panel in the order that you'd like them to appear on the CD. Alternatively, select each file in turn (or shift select) and click on the 'Insert to CD' button above the files in the file panel.
4 I've decided that I want to make a change to the original order. I've transposed tracks 8 and 9 in my selection by dragging Track 9 before Track 8 in the list.

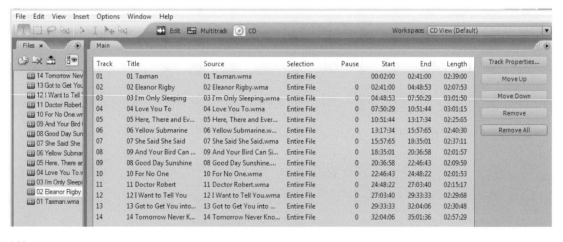

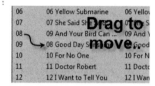

5 Right click on any selection and choose 'Track Properties' from the Right Click menu or choose the track properties button on the left of the main panel.

6 The Track Title and Artist information will be read by any player that can read CD Text. Choose to place a standard 2.00 second pause between tracks or the tracks will appear to run into each other.

7 Repeat for all the tracks in the selection.

8 Choose File, Save CD List to save the selection and properties of that session.

The finished selection can now be printed (burned) to the CD. Because the selection contains Microsoft Windows encoded WMA files, these have to be converted back to wav file format in order to comply with the Red Book standard for linear encoded wav files at 44.1kHz and 16 bit. Dithering and

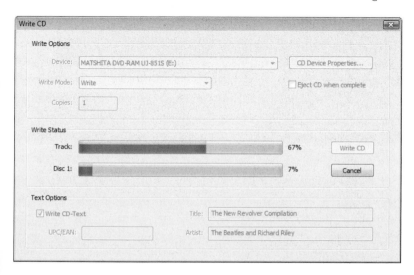

upsampling is automatic but enough space must be available on the volume housing the Adobe Audition temporary folder for copies to be made of all the files in the selection.

Click on the Write CD button in the bottom right hand corner of the main panel to start the CD writing process.

CD Text

Adobe Audition 2.0 provides for Track and Album information to be encoded to the CD as CD text. The ability of the recorder and writer to transfer and display this information depends on the equipment used. However, there's no harm in completely filling in the track and artist information as you have no way of knowing where your CD will one day end up.

Creating a CD from an Adobe Audition session

Adobe Audition 2.0 is able to write to CD in two ways; Disc at Once or Track At Once. When printing a CD for pre-mastering by a duplication plant it is vital that the Disc At Once method is used. This is because during the Track At Once method of burning, the laser is switched off and started again. At this time additional two run in and run out blocks and one link block is also encoded to the CD. This is not a problem for ordinary CD readers as the link and run in blocks are ignored. However duplication plants have very sensitive equipment which picks up these blocks as noise. Therefore most CD duplication plants will not master from CD's created using the Track at Once method.

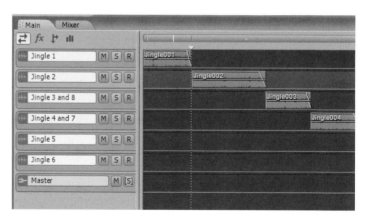

Creating a CD from a multitrack session

Sessions are created when multiple clips are arranged in the multitrack. Effects and balance decisions are made with the mixer and the session is rendered in realtime to audio outputs through the master track on the mixer panel. If the session is to be distributed digitally, or printed to CD the output of the mixer is essentially diverted from the audio output. Instead, a stereo waveform is rendered from the session. The rendered waveform contains all the information and components of the audio session, effects, envelopes and automation. This stereo mixdown becomes the source for the CD Disc At Once session.

I have a collection of radio jingles which I need to compile into a CD to

give to a visiting overseas radio station. The station manager needs an audio
CD to listen to on the way back.

1   I created a session containing my collection of jingles. I'd like to put on a
good show so I've used some clip envelopes to fade some of the
envelopes out and I've deadheaded my jingles using block edge
dragging. I haven't used any mastering effects but I have carefully
balanced my clips using the mixer panel. I've arranged the whole session
to play just as I'd like it to on the CD – including placing two second gaps
between my clips. I haven't used any mastering effects as I'm going to
add these to the mixdown.

2   The session is rendered to a single stereo waveform using File,Export,
Audiomixdown from the menu bar. I've chosen to place the mixdown in
the CD list even though I haven't finished editing yet.

3   The session mix is opened in the edit view window. I haven't placed
markers yet as I prefer to do this in the edit view. Alternatively, markers
can be placed in the multitrack and if non-audio data is saved with the
file they will import into the edit view along with the session. In the edit
view I've added a little widening and Multiband Compression and

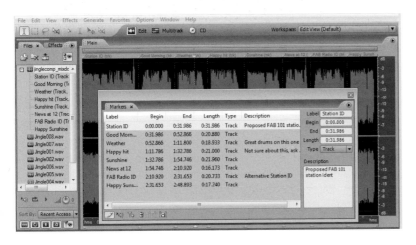

carefully examined and adjusted the envelopes at the beginning and end of each section.

4   A CD track is required for each jingle in my session. Click and drag over the first jingle in the session. The range starts and ends with the music. The two second gap between the jingles is not included in the range. Use Zero Crossings from the File menu to adjust the range inwards and outwards until the range plays seamlessly with no gaps between the start and end of the music and no pops or clicks. Choose Loop Play from the transport to hear the jingle loop repeatedly.

5   When the range is perfect press F8 to create a marker range around the jingle. The range is automatically placed into the Marker Window. Do the same for each of the jingles in the session waveform until you have marker ranges for each track in the session. At the end of the process the stereo mixdown waveform will contain marker ranges for each track and unmarked gaps between tracks.

6   Open the Marker Window (Alt + 8) to see the ranges. By default each range is a cue range. Change the range type to Track for each range and change the track label. Add a description if necessary. Additional index markers can be inserted into the waveform for track index. An index is a marker within the track which is used by some CD players to find positions past the start of the track. These are often used within live music recording where the start of a particular song may not be apparent or in classical and contemporary orchestral music in which musical acts are not announced by a period of silence,

7   Save the finished waveform together with the track marker information. It is necessary to choose the option to save non audio information when saving the file or markers will not be imported into the CD view.

8   Switch to the CD view (Shift + F12)

9   The saved jingle mixdown is now in the file panel. The + icon to the left of the track name indicates that the file has markers. Click on the + sign to see the track ranges saved in the edit view. The ranges will appear under the file name. From here we can either drag individual ranges into the main panel or drag the entire file into the main panel.

Tip

The main panel is also called the selection list. Files and ranges are added to the list and become CD tracks. When individual ranges are dragged into the selection list the CD becomes a Track At Once CD. If a track containing multiple ranges is dragged into the selection you will be prompted to choose between creating a single track CD (Disc At Once) or allow Adobe Audition to expand the file into individual tracks (Track At Once).

---

10 Drag the Jingle mixdown file (not a range) from the files panel into the CD selection. Adobe Audition will detect that the file contains ranges and will ask if the CD is to be Disc At Once or contain individual tracks (Track At Once). This CD is not intended for duplication so I can choose the Track At Once option.

11 The options in the CD Track list can be set to suit my Jingle. Right now I'm not interested in individual track titles so I'll leave that section blank.

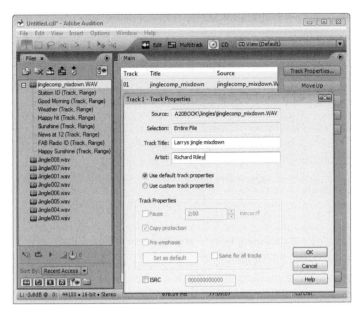

After setting track properties I'll click over the CD Write button in the lower right of the CD view and write the selection to the CD,

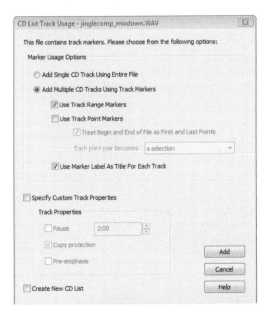

Disc At Once

The station manager might decide that these jingles need to be distributed to all our partners. For this we'll need to send the Adobe CD to a duplication plant who will expect the CD to be written track at once. We already have our session waveform complete with markers so creating the Disc At Once CD is a piece of cake.

1 Create a new CD selection. If necessary, clear the CD selection of all entries (Ctrl + A to select all and press the delete key on the keyboard)
2 Drag the session waveform onto the empty selection list.
3 In the CD List dialog, choose the first option to Add Single CD Track Using Entire File.
4 Press OK

The selection list now simply contains one track. Inside that track are the track ranges and gaps which will create a recognisable CD product. When the CD is written it can be sent to the plant for further processing, duplication and packaging.

ISRC and EAN Codes

Industry Standard Recording Codes are used by broadcasters and rights agencies to identify the source of the CD. A recording can be uniquely identified by its ISRC. Royalty agencies use ISRC codes to automatically assign royalties to copyright holders. ISRC is not a copyrighting or copy protection mechanism. It is not necessary to be a member of a copyright organisation, or to have a record or publishing deal before applying for your own ISRC code key. Adding ISRC numbers to your distributed mixes greatly increases your chances of receiving revenue from your recordings in the wild. Contact Phonographic Performance Limited UK (http://www.ppluk.co.uk) or the IFPI (http://www.ifpi.org) for more information.

ISRC codes are 12 characters long in the form CCXXXYYNNNN.

CC	Country Code
XXX	Three character registrant code
YY	The year of registration
NNNN	A serial number created by the registrant and applied to the recording.

UPC / EAN

This is the Universal Product Code / European Article Number, a numbering system which when combined with a barcode enables the recording to be tracked in retail stores in North America and Canada. The EAN is the European Equivalent of the UPC. The UPC/EAN number may be encoded to the CD.

Labelling the CD with the selection

Currently it's not possible in Adobe Audition to export the selection to a CD labelling product or even a word processor.

Adobe Audition in audio production

This section of the book contains information, hints, ideas and tips on using Adobe Audition 2.0 in the production and finishing of all types of audio.

Finishing and mastering

Music and audio is created to be used in many ways. If the music or audio that you produce is never to be heard outside of your production environment then you can happily discard the rest of this section. On the other hand, as soon as you give a CD of your mix to someone else to play at home you'd better start considering how that music is going to sound not played on your speakers, in your room, through your EQ etc. Even worse – every hifi comes complete with EQ controls designed to completely change the EQ balance of your product. It's like writing a book knowing that your reader will be able to change the structure of your sentence or paragraphs!

Preparing audio for broadcast or distribution

This stereo waveform contains two commercial recordings. The left channel contains a piece of music produced as a radio station ident; a 'jingle'. The right channel is a section of a Neil Young song 'After The Gold Rush' recorded in 1972. Both recordings have considerable commercial acclaim.

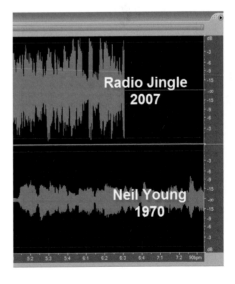

The radio station ident is designed to grab the listener and hold their attention, way after the end of the jingle. A successful jingle writer aims to make recordings that actually sound much better than the commercial songs bookended by the jingles. The radio station needs to keep their audiences because in commercial radio, audience figures fuel the radio stations by means of generating advertising revenue. So the station manager needs to make sure that the audience doesn't want to go anywhere else and programs the station to ensure that audience figures always stay high. This is done by fast cuts, competitions and - more interestingly from our point of view – by lowering the dynamic range of the music that is played.

Dynamic range is the difference between the loudest and the quietest sounds in a recording. The station manager believes that if the audience can't hear the music, they'll go elsewhere. So music is chosen with and broadcasted with the minimum dynamic range possible.

In choosing and broadcasting music with a limited dynamic range the station manager aims to keep the audience concentrating on the station, and be receptive to the adverts.

The difficulty with this policy is that music with restricted range quickly becomes tiring to listen to. It's interesting that the two biggest genres of music to have arisen in the last 15 years are Rap (R&B) and Power Rock/Punk. Both of these genres are distinguished by 'quiet / loud' patterns in the music. The rap vocalist has a very bare bones drum and bass back, leaving the crucial lyrics to come over. The Power Rock/Punk band nearly always has a quiet verse and a contrasting chorus. The contrasting quiet/loud passages are an audio signal and are attractive to the human ear. Both genres are at once 'radio friendly' while keeping their own identity.

This complex arena is now the market for anyone producing audio intended for broadcast. Music must appear as 'good' as the competition. In broadcast terms, 'good' is 'loud'. To compete in the global broadcast markets your productions have to have superhuman qualities.

What is mastering?

When a recording is completed it is mixed down in a number of formats. These include 2.1, 5.1 and stereo. The stereo two track 'print' needs final specialist finishing to prepare it for radio play, CD production or internet delivery. The process of finally equalising and balancing the stereo 'print' is called 'mastering' because the result is a very high quality product which is used as a source for all other products based on that recording. During this process minor EQ problems would be shaved away and gradually mastering engineers became as famous as producers with their own sound and techniques. The term 'mastering' originates from the process of producing a vinyl record. A metal stamp is created from the stereo tape produced by the record producer and used to 'master' the vinyl production run.

Mastering tips

Mastering is applying destructive processes to the finished stereo waveform. This may be an export from the session or an imported waveform. Adobe Audition includes a number of tools which can help you to master your recordings for broadcast, digital distribution or streaming.

The Multiband Compressor

iZotope's Multiband Compressor is a very high quality VST effect. The Multiband compressor separates the frequency into four bands which can each be compressed independently.

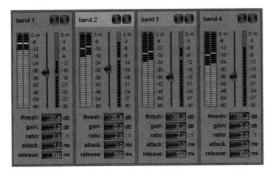 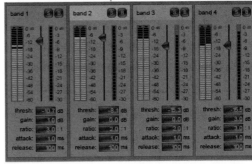

In this session (pic above left) the Multiband Compressor has been set far too low. The low thresholds are pushing the ceiling of the dynamic range right to the floor.

Backing the compressor off to peak just at the very height of the wave-form will enable you to raise the overall level of the track without losing the excitement of the mix (pic above right).

(Top left) the Multiband Compressor has been set far too low. The low thresholds are pushing the ceiling of the dynamic range right to the floor.

(Top right) Backing the compressor off to peak just at the very height of the waveform will enable you to raise the overall level of the track without losing the excitement of the mix.

Tightening the bass in the mix

Use the Multiband Compressor (below left) to add punch to the kick drum by squeezing the low end below 100Hz. Add 3db off gain to this band to emphasise the low end but use the brickwall limiter to keep the output from clipping.

De-essing

De-essing is tightening the bass in reverse. The Multiband compressor can also be used to dip a selection of upper-mid frequencies. This reduces the hard 'ess' sound at the end of sibilant words (below right).

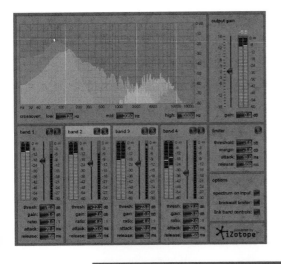 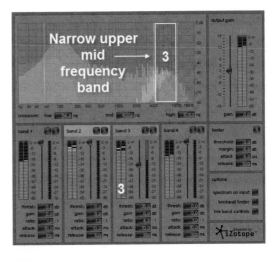

Quote

Sibillant words have hard 'ess' sounds in them. 'Mississippi' is a classic sibilant word.

Parametric EQ

Very few systems are able to process sounds under 40Hz. A high pass filter will shelve the muddy parts of the mix while enabling the important 100Hz frequencies to come through. We perceive bass in the 50 - 100Hz band (left pic).

Remove a selection of high frequencies in the upper wave band to produce 'air' in the mix and calm sibilance (right pic).

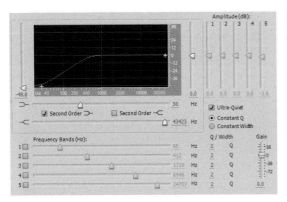 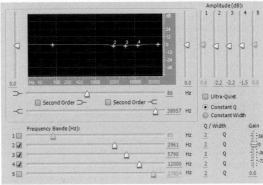

Digital distribution

Bands and artists who sell records al over the world need some way of getting the CD or DVD to the shops. Music industry distributors handle the logistics of collecting CD's from the plant and taking he CD's to the stores where they are sold. This is distribution. Digital Distribution is doing the same thing but rather than getting the CD to the store, the distributor places the CD on line. On Line stores such as iTunes, Napster, etc. don't need packaging or bags but they do need product.

It used to be that distribution wasn't anything that the artist or producer needed to worry about. The record company that signed the artist would handle the distribution and (depending on the kind of deal you may have been foolish enough to sign) would charge some or all of the costs against your share of the profits. Artists and producers now share the same space. Tunes achieve worldwide sales without seeing the inside of the record company boardroom. This is great but comes with a new set of problems. The artist/producer/distributor now needs to not only write and record the song but also to get it to the store. And, music for some kinds of digital distribution needs to be finished with digital distribution in mind.

Finishing for MySpace, YouTube and other digital downloads

This spectral view shows high amplitude frequencies all across the spectrum.

Audio intended for streaming needs to be bright and wide. More Multiband Compression than normal might be used to ensure that your music has enough punch to make it out of laptop speakers or headphones. Smaller speakers also can't produce the same kind of bass as a larger speaker. Pay particular attention to the lower frequencies. Steepen the high pass filter to crossover at a higher point than usual (60Hz instead of 40Hz).

The Karma Equaliser is a free download from KarmaFX. The EQ is particularly good among all these VST effects and the Shine On preset produces a great curve for streaming audio. http://www.karmafx.net

Auto-recovery

Adobe Audition is one of the few audio applications to feature reliable auto-recovery. Computer crashes are inevitable but if Adobe Audition or the supporting operating system should crash Adobe Audition will attempt (usually successfully) to rebuild the session or loaded waveform using the data stored in the temp file location. A dialog will immediately offer the option to continue the next time Adobe Audition is started. If you don't wish to continue from where you left off or if you think that some effects or EQ settings may be causing the software to crash choose delete to return the session to the last saved state.

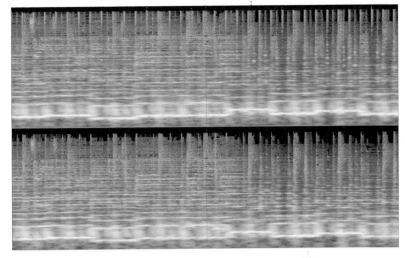

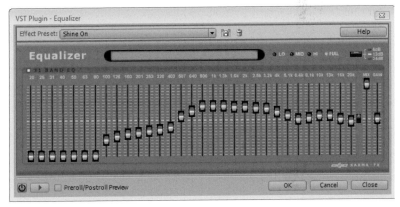

Real time disk space information

Adobe Audition indicates the amount of time taken and memory used on your hard disk in the Status bar underneath the Meter Display. Right clicking over this area, produces a context menu offering time in kilobytes, minutes, second's, and fractions of a second. For best results choose to display the following data.

- Data under cursor
- Sample format
- File Size as data in kilobytes (K)
- Space remaining as time (T)

Using Adobe Audition to create sound

Although recording from external sources is one way to make noise, Adobe

Audition enables the user to create original sounds from scratch using noise or tones, as well as importing audio directly from CD or Quick Time movie. Three sources are used to seed the new waveform; DTMF, Tones and Noise. These are all found under the Generate menu in the edit view.

Generate, DTMF signals (process)

DTMF (Dual Tone Multi Frequency) tones are the noises made by your phone, fax, modem, etc. heard when dialling. The tone is actually two tones; a 'low' tone depending on the horizontal row of buttons and a 'high' tone depending on the vertical row. Tones from 697 to 1633Hz are produced. Adobe Audition also has a DTMF generator. You can test this by entering a phone number and holding the phone receiver to the speakers while the tones are played back. Choose Generate, DTMF Signals (Process) to invoke the DTMF Generator. As they come they are a little dry but can be livened up no end by changing the break time value from the default to a much more exciting 2. Try entering a familiar dial string and experimenting with the tone time and break time values. It's even possible to create rhythmic passages using DTMF as the key.

Generate Noise (process)

Scientific White, Pink or Brown noise generator. White noise is a sound containing random amounts of each frequency within the range of the human ear. White noise is full frequency meaning that every frequency within range (usually 20Hz to 20kHz) is present in equal amounts. Pink noise is filtered to reduce the perceived loudness of the higher frequencies by reducing each octave by 6dB. Brown noise is filtered even further to produce noise that has apparently more low frequency content. Noise may be generated to use as a seed for your own waveforms. For natural sounding wind noise or rain Pink noise is best.

For example, you are asked to provide the sound of wind in trees for a theatrical production:

1 Choose Generate, Noise (process). Produce 10 seconds or so of low intensity (4) pink noise.
2 Apply the Envelope Transform (Effects, Amplitude, Envelope) and choose the ADSR (Attack Delay Sustain Release) preset.
3 Use the graphic page to shape the rise and fall of the wind by dragging the nodes around the graph. Add more nodes by clicking on the line.
4 Choose Spline Curves to produce a natural curve to the noise.
5 Create an EQ curve with the Graphic EQ (Effects, Filters, Graphic EQ) to emphasise more low frequencies.
6 Apply long reverb (Effects, Delay Effects, Reverb) to the entire waveform. You may wish to generate a couple of seconds silence for the end of the waveform to create a realistic reverb tail.

Stand back and wait for the audience applause!

Generate Tones

Generate tones of any length frequency and shape using Generate, Tones, e.g. to produce a low frequency 'throb':

1 Create a new waveform of any length.
2 Choose Generate, Tones and create a 50Hz sine wave.
3 Modulate the wave by 20Hz with a modulation frequency of 8Hz.
4 Choose the first fader and push it to the max. In the general box choose
    Inv Sine as the flavour.
5 Push 'Preview' to hear the low energy machine throb. To turn this static
    throb into a landing spaceship push the 2,3,4,5 faders to 59,46,44,76.
6 Remove the check mark from 'Lock to these settings only' and move to
    the final settings page.
7 On the final settings page make the Base Frequency 20.

Unusual and original samples can be made by modulating noise with tones
or the other way around:

1 Generate two or three seconds of any kind of noise.
2 Press Ctrl + A or choose Edit, Select Entire Wave from the menu bar.
3 Choose Generate, Tones and create any tones.
4 Within the dialog enable any of the modulation options to modulate the
    noise waveform with the tones.

Experiment with different wave shapes and gliding waves to produce creepy
space code noises.

Creating original drum sounds from tones and noise

Use the Generate menu to create brand new sounds from the basic building
blocks of Tone and Noise. It's extremely easy to create a synthetic 303-style
kick drum for instance:

1 Choose File, New and create a empty waveform.
2 Choose Generate, Tones.
3 Create a short gliding sinewave of just .2 seconds starting at 75Hz and
    ending at just 20Hz.
4 Apply an ADSR curve using the Amplitude, Envelope effect.
5 Apply mild distortion using the Effects, Special, Distortion effect. Choose
    the Distort Bass preset.
6 Apply Dynamics Processing. Choose the Power Drums preset.

The same technique may be used to produce a hi-hat sound:

1 Choose File, New and create a empty waveform.
2 Choose Generate, Noise.
3 Generate a short .1-second burst of white noise with a intensity of 12.
4 Create an envelope with a very short tail using Amplitude>Envelope.
5 Use Filters, Parametric EQ to cut the low and mid frequencies.
The contents of the clipboard may be used to modulate a waveform:

1 Choose File, New and create a empty waveform.
2 Choose Generate, Tones.
3 Generate a 1 second Inverse sinewave starting at 600Hz gliding down to 20Hz.
4 Choose File, New and create a second waveform

5 Choose Generate, Noise.
6 Generate a 1 second burst of pink noise with intensity of 5.
7 Copy the entire waveform.
8 Use the Window menu to return to the first waveform called Untitled.
9 Mix paste the Pink Noise over the tone using Overlap and a Volume of 8.
10 Apply Sweeping Phaser over the waveform using the Sweep Highs preset.
11 Apply Reverb using the Dark Drum Plate.
12 Apply Dynamics Processing using the TR909 limit preset.

More about modulation

Two sounds may be modulated either by mix pasting from the clipboard or from within the Generate Tones dialog. Modulation happens when the wave data is multiplied by the current tone settings. The result can be bell like sounds or Vocoder effects depending on the target waveform.

How do I make it do...?

How do I make it give me my effects settings and other settings back?
    Sometimes Audition will dump your effects and other personal settings. These are stored in three .xml files in your Documents folder. The Files are hidden so you'll need to view hidden files and folders to see them.

1 Browse to; C:\Documents and Settings\..name\Application Data\Adobe\Audition\2.0
2 Look for the files; effect_settings.xml, audition_settings.xml and default theme.xml
3 Copy these files to another location.

If Adobe Audition loses your effects and other presets you will be able to retrieve them by copying your saved files back into the default location. If you haven't saved the files first, you won't be able to retrieve your settings.

How can I record from YouTube?

No function exists within Adobe Audition to divert sound from websites into the program. For this feature you'll need to buy additional loopback software which will hook into the soundcard and produce an additional input for Audition.

How can I use Beat Detective within Audition?

Beat Detective is a Protools TDM and is not supported within Audition. However you can use Find Beats and Mark. Within the Edit view choose 'Edit, Auto-Mark, Find Beats and Mark'. While this doesn't offer the rescaling functions of Beat Detective it's easy to use Auto-Mark for detecting individual drum hits within the waveform which can then be exported and re-ordered etc.

How can I make the program keep playing when I click away from it?

An option in preferences prevents Adobe Audition from playing back when another application has focus. Disable this from Edit, Audio Hardware Setup, Release ASIO driver in background. This option should not be enabled.

Glossary

Auto cue
Automatically creates cue ranges based on amplitude information in the waveform.

Auto play
In the Cue List and File Open dialog boxes will play the contents of a wave file before the file is actually loaded.

ASIO
Audio Stream Input / Output. A technology developed by Steinberg for souncard drivers with very little latency.

Bit depth
The number of bits used to store waveform information.

Burning or printing
Recording a CD of your soundtrack by using the CDR drive of your computer. Called burning as the process involves using a low powered laser.

Busses
Output devices for tracks in the Multtrack View. A buss may have many inputs but only one pair of outputs. Used in place of grouping mixer tracks.

CD controls
Transport (stop, playback, etc.) for internal CD player displayed under waveform.

CDROM
Compact disk. Read only method of storage. Can't be overwritten but manufacturing method means data is held permanently.

CD-R
Compact Disk Recordable. Used with CDR drive allows user to 'burn' data to CDR. CDR can only be used once, even though software appears to remove files from CD deleted files still remain and space can't be reclaimed. CDR's must be 'closed'

before disk can be read in a conventional CD drive. CDR is suitable for creating audio CDROM. CD-R can hold about 650mb or 74 minutes of audio data.

CD-RW
Compact Disk ReWritable. Can be written to and overwritten meaning that a single disk may be used many times similar to a floppy disk. However the nature of the read/write process means that a more sensitive drive (often just the home drive) must be used for the read/write process. Hence CD-RW disks are not suitable for distribution of data in any circumstance where the target drive is not known. Equally CD-RW disks are not suitable for audio data. Use CD-R when creating audio disks.

Channel
A waveform may have one or two channels. Mono waveforms have one channel, stereo waveforms have two channels. Channels may be copied from a stereo waveform by clicking the extreme upper or lower edge of the channel before clicking and dragging. To convert a stereo waveform to a mono waveform use 'Convert Sample Type'.

Clipping
Distortion created when the maximum input level to the soundcard exceeds the bit rate used to calculate the sample data. Is reproduced on the waveform as a full amplitude sample and is heard as distortion.

DAW
Digital Audio Workstation.

Direct X
Microsoft software driver.

Display Adapter
Hardware device inside the computer controlling the computer monitor.

Display Range Bar

Solid bar above waveform display in edit view. The length of the bar illustrates the amount of the waveform seen in the current view.

Display Time Window

Window beneath the waveform view with constantly updated figure showing elapsed time in a number of formats.

Drop down box

List box which expands when clicking over small handle to right of box.

DSP

Digital Signal Processor. The PC doesn't have any hardware devoted to DSP in an audio sense but this term is used to describe effects that have been created digitally rather than in the analogue domain.

DVD

Digital Versatile Disc. Is commonly used as a medium for distributing movies but can be used for any digital data.

Edit view

Two channel waveform editor.

Effects

Digital effects created by Adobe Audition.

Effects Racks

Effects groups applied to single tracks in the multitrack view.

Envelopes

Graphical illustration of pan, volume or other data over waveblocks in the multitrack view. Envelopes can be adjusted using the mouse.

EQ

Equalisation or tone controls.

Filters

Filter out frequency ranges e.g: Graphic Equaliser, Phase Shifter.

Frequency range

Variable range of frequencies based around a centre frequency.

Handles or nodes

Small square boxes available for dragging using the mouse. Right click to see data values.

Hard drive

Physical storage device inside the computer.

Impulse

A waveform describing the characteristics of a sound that is overlaid on another waveform during convolution. The second waveform then adopts the characteristics of the first.

Level Meters

Indicate amplitude data received by Adobe Audition from sound card driver.

Loops

Short section of waveform seamlessly repeating.

Menu bar

Drop down list of items.

MIDI

Musical Instrument Digital Interface. A LAN protocol adopted by the music industry for sending and receiving data between PC's.

MP3

System of encoding waveform to produce very high quality sound using extremely small file sizes. The standard for distribution of audio over the web.

MTC

MIDI Time Code. A method of sending timing information between MIDI capable devices.

Multitrack sound card

Physical hardware device inside the computer featuring more than one pair of inputs and outputs.

Multitrack view

Shows arrangements of waveblocks in tracks. Tracks are played in synchronisation and so waveblocks on different tracks can be overlaid to create multitrack audio.

Noise

White noise contains an equal proportion of all frequencies. Brown and Pink noise is weighted towards the low frequencies.

Panel

A container for either a mixer, file, effect or any other object. Panels can be tabbed inside a frame.

Playback cursor (Start Time indicator)

Shows current position of playback in the waveform.

Plug In

Third party software hosted by Adobe Audition. Typically additional effects software.

RAM

Random Access Memory. Physical storage inside the computer.

Range or selected area
Selection of the waveform created by dragging the mouse over any area.

Red Rover
USB control device. Created by Syntrillium. A set of transport controls and multitrack information set into a small remote control.

Ripping
Digital extraction of audio data from pre-recorded CD's.

Ruler Bar
Calibrated ruler below the waveform display indicating time or any number of other formats.

Sampling rates
Expressed as frequency. CD quality audio is made of samples reproduced 44,100 times per second. In other words there are 44,100 individual samples in every second of waveform data at that frequency rate.

SMPTE
Society Of Motion Picture Technical Engineers. Body behind the SMPTE timecode method of synchronisation.

Snapping
Playback cursor is attracted to area of ruler bar or other choices in Edit>Snapping menu. Makes precise positioning of playback cursor much easier.

Sound card
Physical device inside the computer able to convert audio into digital data.

Spectral View
Displays waveform as frequency rather than amplitude.

Status Bar
Area in the extreme lower right of the program window. Contains text fields showing data relating to available storage space, etc. Right click over this area to see more options.

Temp files
Data created by Adobe Audition at program time and stored temporarily on hard drive.

Timecode
MTC (MIDI Time Code) or SMPTE timecode is read and generated by Adobe Audition and so is able to synchronise with external machines such as VCR or reel tape multitrack machines.

Tones
Sinewave or other wave types at fixed or varying frequencies.

Toolbars
Small button bars above waveform display. Buttons duplicate menu bar items and may be removed. Right click over button bar to view options.

Track controls
Small controls to left of each track in multitrack view. Contains controls for output and recording device, mute solo and pan etc.

Track properties
Volume, pan and other values available by right clicking on any free space in track controls to produce floating window or in table form through Track Mixers.

Tracks (in multitrack view)
Waveblocks in multitrack view are laid out in tracks to enable many waveblocks to be played at the same time.

Transport bar
Button bar containing VCR style controls for controlling playback functions.

YMMV
Your Mileage May Vary. In other words the complexity and variables associated with computer systems of all sorts means that a simple statement such as 'add more RAM for better performance' takes on extra meaning. The results I get may be different to the results you get. Hence 'Your Mileage May Vary'.

Wav
Shortened term for waveform used as file name suffix in Windows.

Waveblock
Contains waveform data in multitrack view but crucially doesn't change data of source waveform. Waveblocks may be moved, deleted, trimmed etc. without affecting original recording.

Waveform
Computer representation of sound as data.

WDM
Windows Driver Model. WDM drivers are compatible across all Microsoft Windows operating systems. The object of WDM drivers is to make it much easier for vendors to develop and support their products without having to write a different driver for each Windows OS.

Appendix
An introduction to digital concepts

A basic understanding of some digital audio concepts and terms is vital when using audio software such as Adobe Audition. The following is a very useful forum post which clearly explains and defines some of the terms used in this book.

Very many thanks go to Bob Weitz for permission to use the following section, originally posted to the DPS24 forum at Vibestudio. Bob is based in Los Angeles where he has been a sound engineer in the movie business for nearly 20 years, member of IATSE local 700. In 1998 (along with his partner, Dan Leimeter) Bob was honoured with a Technical Achievement Award from the Academy of Motion Picture Arts and Sciences for advancements in the design of tools for optical sound alignment. Bob is also an active musician and home recording buff.

Decibel (dB)

A decibel is 1/10 of a bel. Originally, the bel was called a Transmission Unit (TU), which was used by Bell Telephone to quantify signal loss over long telephone lines. The decibel is more commonly used, since it is a smaller unit, making finer measurements more convenient.

Decibels use a base-10 logarithmic scale to express the ratio of a signal or sound level to a reference level. 0 dB doesn't mean 'no signal', it means 'no difference' compared to the reference. A doubling of power is +3 dB, a doubling of amplitude or voltage would yield four times the power, or + 6 dB. -3 dB would mean half the power, which corresponds to 0.707 times the voltage.

Standard reference Levels for analog audio

0 dBm = 1 milliwatt of power into a 600 ohm load = 0.775 V rms. (old school, from the days of matched impedences and power transfer)

0 dBu = 0.775 V rms, unloaded or no load specified (modern voltage standard derived from the dBm standard)

0 dBV = 1.0 V rms (usually used in unbalanced, consumer audio)

Common nominal analog audio Levels for 0 VU (volume units)

+4 dBu = 1.228 V rms (the most common pro audio signal level, usually balanced line)

-10 dBV = 0.316 V rms (the most common consumer audio level, usually unbalanced)

Headroom

The difference between nominal level and the maximum undistorted level. This is usually expressed as a positive number, the distortion ceiling in dB above nominal level. Example: nominal level of +4 dBu and a maximum undistorted level of +22 dBu will yield Headroom of 18 dB.

Signal-to-noise ratio

The difference between nominal level and the noise floor. This is usually expressed as a negative number, the noise floor in dB below nominal level. Example: nominal level of +4 dBu and a noise floor of -60 dBu will yield a signal-to-noise ratio of -64 dB.

Dynamic range

The difference between the maximum undistorted level and the noise floor. This is usually expressed as a positive number, the entire range including signal-to-noise ratio and Headroom in dB. Example: noise floor 0f -60 dBu and a maximum undistorted level of +22 dBu will yield a Dynamic Range of 82 dB.

The meter scale is different in the digital domain because the meters are usually faster acting than the old VU meters, and are calibrated with 0 dB as full-scale (0 dBfs). All measurements are taken as negative numbers, dB below full scale (maximum unclipped signal). Commonly, a digital level of -20 dBfs corresponds to 0 VU, and will yield an analog output of +4 dBu. This would indicate Headroom of 20 dB.

In 16-bit resolution, the noise floor is theoretically at -96 dBfs, indicating a signal-to-noise ratio of -76 dB, and a total dynamic range of 96 dB.

Index